Indian Women Across Generations

INDIAN WOMEN ACROSS GENERATIONS

UMA NARULA

ATLANTIC
PUBLISHERS & DISTRIBUTORS

Published by
ATLANTIC
PUBLISHERS & DISTRIBUTORS
B-2, Vishal Enclave, Opp. Rajouri Garden,
New Delhi-110027
Phones : 25413460, 25429987, 25466842

Sales Office
7/22, Ansari Road, Darya Ganj,
New Delhi-110002
Phones : 23273880, 23275880, 23280451
Fax : 91-11-23285873
web : www.atlanticbooks.com
e-mail : info@atlanticbooks.com

ISBN 81-269-0413-5

Printed in India
at Nice Printing Press, Delhi

Dedicated To

Women in my Life

My Mother: Surinder Kanta

My Daughter: Ameeta Soni

My Grand-daughter: Tara Soni

CONTENTS

LIST OF FIGURES

PROLOGUE

No exposure to outside world, No media, No telephone, No neighbourhood, No friends, but helpless, powerless, and dominated by males. That is the picture of the Indian women in nineteenth century.

There were the painful memories of my grandmother cloistered at home. Anger at my mother's life when she could not go to school, when she could not enjoy her childhood frolicking around with her playmates but only peep through the veils. Her helplessness in not being able to control producing a large number of children. My anger and struggle to be on equal footing with professional male colleagues; many of whom were not intellectually and professionally better than me and yet were enjoying promotions all the time. The younger generation of today consolidated on our sacrifices and they did accept the challenge. They are assertive, aggressive and are competitive to be in the male mainstream but certainly on their own terms.

The pain, anger, helplessness, and mental turmoil of women of the bygone eras; the anger, assertiveness of the present age—all put together created new identity for women.

In retrospect, it seems my mother's generation was honest and had the ability to describe their pain, helplessness, and restlessness but they never had the freedom, opportunities to work out on their capabilities. Her childhood was a model of how conventions can imprison the spirit of woman and make her miserable. Every woman lived two genres. My mother in her later life achieved a social status and an identity because of changing times. She had a clear message for the coming generations—be independent economically as well as socially; make your own way; and achieve your own identity. Her strength throughout this experience was reinforced by the efforts of the social activists, national governmental efforts through legislation and efforts by the international communities to boost human rights of women.

This was significant for me. I wanted to research the 'roots' of women's generations to assess the significance of this message, to perceive the possibilities, and opportunities open to women when the male society had the power to limit women self-development. I wanted to know about the forces which goaded women to act against the currents of their times. I presumed there has to be some condition in women's life which insulates them from society's expectations and give them strength, energy, and a sense of destiny which will not permit them to accept conventional female roles.

I felt the compelling need to write about the discriminations and denials to women in the past and present in the particular areas of activities. In the process, I got interested to chronicle the struggles and achievements of the generations highlighted through their experiences. The personal scenarios bring to the fore the predicament of women. The study derives much of its strength and sophistication from the basis of women's experiences of oppression who continued to experience daily exclusions of various kinds.

We relive and recover experiences by writing about women generations. As E.M. Forster said, "...only connect and you will be astonished at the events of your life, recovered on the screen or page weave themselves into patterns of unexpected understanding." When we focus our vision on the incidents, the limits give us the opportunity to dig within that limited experience to see "What may not have been noticed before when we were living those events. The connections reveal unexpected meanings." The act of writing those experiences of generations not only give us insights but also brings forth contradictions, doubts, and new ideas.

The family stories about our grandmothers and mothers bind us to one another when distances and circumstances would otherwise drive us apart. These family stories are the personal stakes that mark us as unique family. The stories keep memories burning. Partly as mythology, and partly as guidebook, they preach the importance of resilience in the face of hardship, the honour of standing up to new challenges, and even the folly of depending too much on men! They are the grandinetti family values passed down to the generations with lessons learnt.

This book traces the evolution of sensibilities of women across generations in India since 1900. It is the story of survival and growth of women over a century, which epitomizes continuity and change. The issues of identity of women, societal, and cultural strictures inhibiting women's full formation of self-hood, had been the uppermost during this evolutionary period. The book offers the analytical interpretations of attitudes and behaviour of these women across generations through the analysis of their experiences and actions.

The year 1900 is the cut-off date for our sample. Our sample includes women who are octogenarians (in eighties). Not only they talk about themselves but also they recall about their mothers and their grandmothers, daughters and grand-daughters. We have narratives from women in sixty plus age-group and those in twenty plus group. Thus, the women of the nineteenth and twentieth centuries are discussed in these narratives.

The women subjects unfold the events of their lives and chronicle the sequences of their attitudes and behaviour, their interpretations and judgments about them, and the protests and the struggles that they have undergone to magnify their voices overtime.

The women who have contributed to this book are very special. They have given us generations' glimpses by honest accounts of their lives, and by articulation of their experiences.

On the eve of 90s, crucial questions are posed to women in all age groups who comprise our sample. How are women to achieve without becoming a part of the male mainstream? These are supported by their own experiences.

This book presents a unique perspective. We assume that women have come a long way since a century back though all development is not positive in all cultures. We also assume that some of these developments are culture specific at a particular point of time; and others may be universally applicable. *Indian Women Across Generations* is the story of Indian women and it highlights their generations' puzzles.

—Uma Narula

ACKNOWLEDGMENTS

My foremost thanks are to those contributors who have given honest accounts of their own life, perceptions, and their experiences with other women across generations. These narratives developed the evolutionary story of women across generations since a century back and that is the focus of this book.

My thanks to other intellectual discussions groups in India and America who enriched the study by their valuable insights and suggestions.

Most of all, my children Ameeta and Vivek need special thanks for inspiring me for professional active writing and critical comments on the manuscript. My grandchildren Atul and Tara need thanks for being co-operative and patient.

—Uma Narula

1

INDIAN WOMEN ACROSS GENERATIONS

There is a new world somewhere
They call it a Promise Land
And I will be there someday
If you hold my hand. *Anonymous*

We sought our memories not only for expression of female despair and constriction of older generations but also to proclaim the possibilities of life for women as human beings who do not have to take their identity from men in their lives.

The study across generations is umbilical line study. Umbilical line is defined as that unique matrilineal ancestral line which passes back only through our mother—and her mother—and her mother—and her mother....and so on. But our study is neither genealogical nor genetic; rather we trace women development process.

The generation theory deals with three notions about generation. One, the European intellectuals thought the generations have a regular rhythm of three to a century. Two, modern demographers define generations in terms of thirty years or the approximate time it takes a female to replace herself by giving birth to a daughter. Three, we deal with five generations in a century as there is overlapping of genres.

What makes a generation?

A generation is something that happens to people; it is like a social class, or an ethnic group people are born into, it does not depend on the agreement of its members. Even people who disagree will perceive that they share a common self-awareness and a common destiny. A group's collective self-identity can become so powerful, so compelling, that it not only binds together its own members but also draws older and younger generations to its particular *Weltanschauung*.

The second assumption is that generation is the primary agent of social change. Each generation is born in a time it shares with no other and is product of a life experience it shares with no other. At first the vital sensibilities i.e. the aggregate values and aspirations of a rising generation may be dominated by an older and more powerful generation ahead of it. But as the older generation passes, the younger generation is able to carry its own worldview into adulthood. Reform is thus brought organically into a society. People do not change, generations do. The life of prominent individuals within a generation cannot stand apart from the generation itself. If they are the fish, then masses are sea in which they swim. The generation sensibility they share is far more significant than the things that separate them.

The third assumption is that the impact of a generation whether on the individuals within it, or on the larger culture is directly related to the size of the population. The demographers take generation as a cohort. The size of a cohort is a force that shapes its life. If successive generations are of comparable size there is orderly transition of power. But if there is generation imbalance, the delicate watchworks of society can be jammed. If an older generation finds themselves outnumbered by the young, socialization can break down.

These assumptions—that a generation is worth study, that a generation is the carrier of social change, and that the size of a generation is its most crucial characteristic sets us to study women across generations in 20th century.

Every generation insists on its own uniqueness, believing its experiences to be most stressful than that of any other generation before it. The real question is whether the changes we observe around us are particular to the times or to a generation.

The unique perspective of each generation gives us *insights* into life experiences of that particular generation, and the challenges they face. Further, the life experiences of subsequent generations present the impact of process of social change that they have undergone. Each generation lives two genres of experiences—the early life experiences that are greatly influenced by the environment of the immediate older generation of the mother; then as they grow older, they face the challenges of their own generation.

Each generation in particular culture face different insights and challenges. Therefore, the generation challenges are very culture-specific.

There are three frameworks in which the experiences of generations are evaluated. One, development communication framework which focuses on women development through generations by national and international efforts, and interventions by non-government organizations (NGOs). Second, the feminists communication framework that focus on social movements in which a variety of social actors seek to create a new social reality, a new social culture, a new logic for all aspects of life including technology. Third, women take their own initiatives to develop discourses which starts from the analysis of their social reality and leads to involvement in their struggles.

The basic approach of all three frameworks is *Conscientization* that focuses on communication and education; awakening the individual consciousness to her situation of oppression, educating her by community communication and activation, or by organized process of social change. The recognition of oppression leads the individual or group to become the agents of change, breaking the culture of silence, and engaging in social actions and group initiatives.

The introductory chapter provides background about women in general and about Indian women in particular. It highlights Images of women; Paradigms of generational change *vis-a-vis* social change; women's participation in 'movements' and politics; and the national and international efforts to develop them over these ten decades.

Paradigm of Generational Change

The role played by women throughout generations is four tiers: reproductive (child bearing and rearing), productive (as secondary income earners through informal activities), productive primary earners, household and community management.

The paradigm of generational change among women gives us interesting insights. The octogenarian women in eighty plus age group generation were passive and they quietly endured the sufferings, despair and depression. They did not recognize the pain inherent in the lack of selfhood. Why did they resist recognizing their own suffering or feel guilty if they perceive it? The important point was that they failed to articulate it for fear of loosing male protection.

The next generation of my mother started the process to change their sufferings and constrictions by articulating their pain and sufferings but avoided risk, adventure, and opportunities.

The generation of sixty plus age group transformed that suffering by organized efforts to avoid suffering, and constrictions; and also to insulate themselves against it.

I have a sense that passivity, helplessness, powerlessness of earlier generations made mine and coming younger generations more ambitious, restless, achieving, assertive and aggressive.

The women who did have the courage, self-confidence, and autonomy to achieve and made their way in the male dominated world in the subsequent generations did so by identifying themselves with male ideals and role models. This could have sounded ideal initially. But the moot question is should they follow the male models or carve their own models?

The struggles for inequality were/are more difficult because it is not a struggle against an outside enemy but against their brothers, fathers, husbands, and comrades.

Process of Social Change

There are five specific ways in which women of third world countries are analyzed. It constructs the women as a homogeneous powerless group located as victims. The category of analysis is the mode of defining women in terms of their object status i.e. the way in which they are affected or not affected by certain institutions and systems. The five categories project women as: (i) victims of male violence—physical violence, such as beating, rape, sexual assault, sexual oppression, and genital circumcision etc. The focus is the male who perpetuates it and woman who defends herself; (ii) women as universal dependents. Women's place in social life is not in any direct sense a product of the things she does; but the meanings her activities acquire through concrete social interactions; (iii) both positive and negative impact of colonial process; (iv) women and familial systems. Women as women are not located within the family; rather it is in the family that women are constructed as an effect of kinship structures of being mother, sister, daughter, and wife; (v) women as target of religious ideologies. Women oppression is a global phenomenon. Many a times women in third world countries are required to postpone their needs and their rights again and again for the greater cause of nationalism. The process of social change occurs within the framework of these categories.

We sense and visualize change among women: a change in their lifestyles, their philosophies of life, their ways of doing and thinking about things. The life perspectives have changed and are changing. This process of social change and development pertaining to Women across Generations has changed women. This is true perhaps across all cultures. The social activists, individuals in families, women themselves have contributed towards such change. Besides the individual efforts to change, the national and international governments have made tremendous efforts and spent resources to develop women across generations.

The process of social change has been gradual across women generations in different areas. The change has been more noticeable in the areas of education, career choices, marriage choices, health, recreation, socialization, human, and social rights etc. These have reflected in the overall lifestyles of women of every generation—their mannerisms, behaviour, values, ways of doing and thinking, set of attitudes and beliefs, language and conversation styles, and even in modes of dress and hairstyles. These profiles are very generation specific. Every generation has lived a unique life perspective. History repeats itself and so do the generation specific lifestyles and perspectives. The generations are interconnected by these connections and by reinterpretations of the past.

In earlier generations of 1900; in the family structure, the women did the nurturing of children at home but the males were the representatives for the outer world. So much so that women had no say in decisions made about children's education, career, marriages, and their social interactions with the community.

Freudian psychoanalysts suggest woman's longing for sons as expression of the masculine part of herself—played in an acceptable way. But I do not know how this theoretical assumption was true and applicable to the Indian society of those times. Indian women did have intense desire and preference to have sons, aversion to have girls (because they identified girls with their own sufferings) but they had no role to play in molding the sons! Therefore, fathers were always the role models.

But subsequent generations did change. Now parenting and nurturing are done by both the parents of today. The change over was due to development of general inclination of parents to share active part in molding their children. Fathers also share parenting and nurturing due to women working outside home. The results of such change in these areas brought in economic independence; and social, economic, and political empowerment for women to shape their lives. Over a period of time, new issues have also cropped up such as impact of new economic policies on women, political participation of women, portrayal of women in media, impact of communalism on women, new legislation—new legal issues, and legal protection of women, and increasing crimes against women.

2

WOMEN IMAGES: DYNAMIC FORCES

When women talk, they project many images—both positive and negative images of women generations. The definition of positive-negative image has undergone change overtime and whatever was a positive image way back may not be so now.

The images may vary. There is wide assortment of current images about women. One image is of a superwoman as presented in the media and that of a simple human machine. Another image projects women being independent economically and with lots of empowerment in many areas of life. Freedom for women will have no meaning unless she has the power and the good sense to relate it to. The negative image may be of women being the focus of various crimes and exploitations manipulated by men.

There is a tendency to define women in monolithic terms and associate women with notions of passivity, victimization, and isolation. On the contrary women may be viewed as diverse subjects and social actors, as heterogeneous groups with different experiences of subordination (Pillar Riano 1994).

One way of becoming the creators of our own images—the images that correspond to our true identity and not to a model of woman which may not represent us—is to begin defining ourselves from the inside. We cannot diminish the importance of women's images. An image is a means of knowing and we can help change ourselves through knowing these images. At the individual level this is a part of self-exploration and discovering of voice of the valuation of individual. In the group context, because of social change goals, these images operate as bridges for collective history, implying and bringing together the multiplicity of individual perspectives and experiences. Thus building of a commonsense through differences and commonality. Women create spaces, texts, and images for encoding their history. That impact strengthens self-expression, recognition, and esteem of women.

Figure 2.1 shows the predominant women images, the dynamic forces that create those varied positive and negative images, and the need for strategies to deal with them.

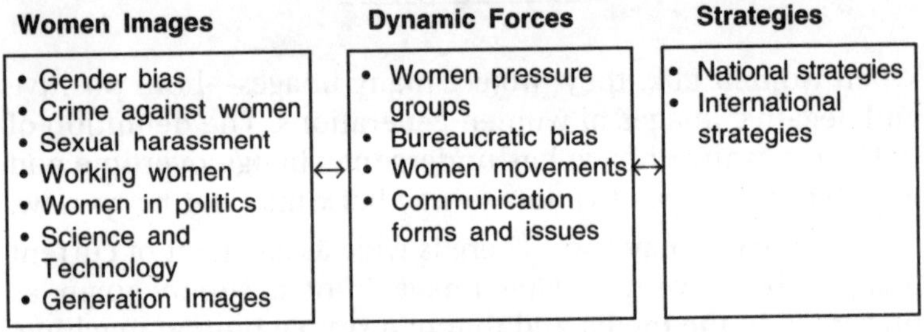

Fig. 2.1: Women Images.

The predominant images are of gender bias and discrimination in the competitive world of today. One of such image is that emerging technologies have more male gender perspectives; that there is gender predominating dimensions of development. The most predominant image is that women issues are debated by men and put in practice by governments and organizations where there are no women.

The question of media image of women is of importance. Though the media portrays itself as neutral, its impact is rarely neutral. The power of media image can be used either to reinforce harmful stereotypes about women or be a vehicle for progress and inclusion. The key to improving women image in the media is to involve more women communicating information about women issues as writers, news broadcasters, and other media professionals. Women need greater access to decision-making roles to ensure that the information being transmitted reflects the wide experiences of women on their issues. The assumption is that media content and images covering women issues and gender portrayal will change for better if women are involved in its production. Women media professional can change the ways in which established issues are covered.

The other interesting image is that men predominate all the 'hard news' that includes economics, politics, labour, war and its strategies, social development and movements etc. The 'soft news' or women related issues are negligible in news reports suggesting women seldom appeared in newscasts. When they do, they are presented in stereotyped roles, with unidentified professional status, they are portrayed as suffering victims and with gender bias.

More important and harder is to vigil against the bitterness for male colleagues who had harmed and discriminated women, or the professional slights on them because they happened to be women. When women happened to be a victim of time and people (Conference Feb. 1996, New Delhi).

Personal Law and Women's Rights. In India in 1947, the religious minorities were given the assurance that their personal laws shall be protected by specific provisions embodied in the Indian Constitution. Recently in May 1996 the public debate in parliament on the issue of cultural nationalism has veered round to accepting legal pluralism in family laws as a necessary condition of cultural pluralism, provided the demands of women's rights to equality and justice are met within the community based personal laws.

Democratic rights groups are more concerned about issues of gender justice than uniformity. Part of this shift on focus lies on the widespread acceptance of cultural pluralism as an important issue on human rights agenda.

Should the unitary cultural net include marriage, divorce, maintenance, inheritance, succession, and guardianship? The fact is that a major part of the civil code applies commonly to all citizens. It is only in the area of intimately culture-bound family life that community-based laws differ not only among the religious minorities but also among the diverse social groups. Legal pluralism in matrimonial laws is practiced in USA too where different states have varying divorce laws. Such legal pluralism in family matters is increasingly introduced in other western countries to provide people with freedom to choose how they would constitute the family including contractual marriages. The issue never gets linked with national unity and solidarity.

It is argued that if the strategy of gender justice accommodates plural cultural norms, a common struggle for women's rights can generate more social cohesiveness and human integration than an abstract uniformity of family laws. For example, under the broader issue of human rights, a divorcee's right to a share in the matrimonial home and other properties needs to be promoted.

It is a pity there is no organized movement in India for Muslim women for required reforms within the framework of Islamic value system to outlaw the unilateral instant divorce just by saying three times—talak, talak, talak (divorce); and unfettered male right to polygamy.

Kalim Bahadur (1997) commenting on the complexity of women's social status in Pakistan argues that most fundamentalist groups in Pakistan have interpreted Koranic teachings with an anti-women tilt. The two recent remarkable judgments in Pakistan High Court upheld the right of the woman to arrange her marriage on her free Will. Pakistan's Shariat courts whose interpretations of Islamic laws is constitutionally binding on the High Courts held that adult sane women had the free right to marriage. At the same time another judge of the same High Court annulled a woman's marriage on the ground that it had been sanctified without the consent of the guardian.

There is discrimination in education, employment. They are against coeducation, there is ban on women's participation in sports. It has the lowest female literacy rate in the world.

Most Islamic scholars maintain that women have been given high status in Islam. However in actual practice their position has declined overtime because of local customs, arbitrary interpretations, and male chauvinism.

Pakistan Human Development Center Report (April 1997) reveals that women suffer worse discrimination in seven countries of South Asia (Bangladesh, India, Pakistan, Sri Lanka, Bhutan, Nepal and Maldives) than any part of the world. To be a woman in South Asia is to be a non-person. The report further highlights the mistreatment of women; from cradle to grave there is preferential treatment for boys and litany of violence against women—from infanticide to child abuse, to rape, to dowry deaths, and to pyre-burning. Neglect of women in South Asia is directly linked to economic status. It had the lowest ratio of female administrators and managers—only 3%. Such indices of gender-disparity persist in a region where four out of seven countries India, Pakistan, Bangladesh, and Sri Lanka boast of female head of the government at present or in the recent past.

Women must involve in movements focusing on their issues because the stereotype of women speaking through the mouths of men has got to stop.

The First Wave of the women's movements in the world started with women's suffrage and other pioneers of the 19th century. The Second Wave was the women's liberation movements of 60's and 70's that demanded equal rights and opportunities. The ethos of the Third Wave springs from 30 years of feminism's shortcomings and unfinished business, as well as its achievements. The Third Wave is fueled by a different kind of anger than of women's liberation movements of a generation ago. Third Wave acknowledges their foremother's victories.

Why a Third Wave is needed? The 60's created a new way of life. If the 60's were an era of conflicts, the 90's is an era of contradictions. From evolutionary and revolutionary point of view, Third Wave is made of women who felt less of oppression of the Second Wave. The Third Wave women have seen public women in dominance. These women have no recollection of the struggle for equal rights. The generation 'X' of Third Wave looks for cultural rather than political feminism. This is a big shift. This generation has grown up transgender, bisexual, interracial etc. We find ourselves creating identities that accommodate ambiguous and our multiple personalities.

As with any social movement, personal experience is central.

There are four stages of women movements. One, raising awareness among women about their physical, psychological, and social afflictions in general. Two, creating awareness, orientation, and action about specific issue (affliction). Third, action oriented steps such as public discourses, public demonstrations, segmented appeals, representations etc. to focus the issue and create solutions. Fourth, implement solutions through legal actions and social reforms. All the four stages involve, consistent efforts of women and their support systems; the legal protection from the governmental systems; and social protection from the non-governmental systems.

Why women movements fail? There are both general and culture specific reasons. There are two strategies responsible for failure: Tokenism and bonding females with males. Tokenism allows males to use women to protect themselves against the claim for equal representation in their ranks. Males discover that they can isolate women from other women, from women causes, and from identification with women by co-opting radicals.

Secondly, whatever is the nature of injustice women do not show solidarity with support systems and network among themselves for their own causes and rarely encourage female autonomy. Though these support systems and networks have mostly operated effectively in the crisis of conventional womanly life areas such as birth, weddings, death, imposed loneliness etc.

Thus failure of women's movements are attributed to four factors, (i) failure of women to bond, (ii) failure to imagine women as autonomous, (iii) failure to resist male protection to enter male mainstreams, (iv) failure to find own support systems to stand for their own issues and nurture their concerns.

When women movements have a focus issue then the efforts are to bond women together to support it, to force men to support it, and provide solutions if they (women) are the targets. This happens in issues such as dowry demands, violence, crime protection etc. Impersonal efforts are made such as legal protection, and implementation of social reforms.

Bonding women support for their own causes is the main problem as they continually undermine their ability to bond under social and psychological pressures.

The negative image is that women themselves ensure that women do not get what they deserve. Who cannot overlook the harsh mothers-in-law in India or Pakistan torturing the young brides, or burning them in greed for more dowry, encouraging their sons to beat their wives. Even at times marriages will break as mothers are possessive of their sons.

There are always indigenous roots for social movements. Women organizations and media productions are involved in larger social movements that use protest, economic survival, defense of rights, and social demands for change to activate women as social communicative agents to perpetuate women's key roles as equal partners in the process of change.

There are feminist concerns about manipulative capacity of mass media to foster gender inequalities and the other approach is to question inequalities as a strategy to defend life in conditions of political and economic hardships.

The younger generation of today present diverse images. They are torn between the old values and new and supposedly better ways. The stress of work place, economic and social change, combining foursome roles of homemaker, mother, wife, and career women have transformed old patterns of family living. As a result there is more stress and general disorganization. It is the woman who suffers in the deal. Demands of their daily marathon deprive them of enjoying small pleasures of life, nurturing family relationships. Racing against time, full of ambitions, and competitive life; they have more worries and troubles to face. Thus there is more social stress.

Younger generation of women are shattering industry's glass ceiling. The new executives overcome stereotypes and demands.

As for the image of working women, for over a generation, mothers at office, mothers at home have been hunkered down. They have not been always comfortable with their own decisions about work and family but they have been defensive in the presence of others. It is a notion that women can and do have choices. But these choices are also weighted by outside forces.

One such important force, in many developed countries (USA, Canada, Sweden) is the social policy of taxing wives' incomes jointly with the husbands. On one hand, women are forced to work to pay for higher quality of life for the family, and to pay for the higher taxes, but on the other hand the tax laws favour single-earner families. They have a built-in prejudice against working mothers. Average working wife's salary is lost to taxes and work-related expenses. Part-timers may be working at a loss.

When filing joint tax returns with husband, woman as the secondary earner is taxed at a higher rate. At the lowest level a bias against the two-worker family is bias against families themselves. For the middle class, it makes hard personal choices and still harder economic choices. Middle class women are placed between rock and a hard place. They are not making that much net money. They can stay home and avoid stresses, then they sacrifice earnings. They can go to work, but it is very stressful and the net money gain is nothing.

Thus the tax structure can push families into traditional roles than they may wish. For example, when a family needs to raise money, it often makes more economic sense for the husband to work for longer hours than for the wife to work part time. Economic sense and common sense collide. We want a more balanced life between men and women, work and family. It is time to right the tax prejudice. Let wives' salary be taxed less by filing tax returns individually!

There are many developing countries (India, Pakistan, and Bangladesh) which encourage women to work both for economic necessity and economic independence; and to develop and count them as major work force. As tax incentives these women file individual tax returns, they get more tax shelters, and as compared to men higher income limit exemptions for taxation.

Study finds bureaucracy biased against women. Indian Administrative Service (IAS) and Indian Foreign Service (IFS) in charge of implementing the country's 'gender neutral' policies, predominately remains a male bastion composed of stereotypical males who believe that women do not make ideal officers. The survey conducted by Lal Bahadur National Academy of Administration reveals. The general perception of largely male officers is that ideal worker is the one whose concentration is on full time job while his wife or other woman takes care of his personal needs and his children. The study says the women officers are presumed to have legitimate obligations such as child bearing, home-keeping, which are other than those required by their jobs. This is an implicit assumption that the woman's place is within the confines of a home and that career is viewed as an additional activity.

The survey concludes that women respondents recounted that there are innumerable instances of subtle prejudice against women in the services. The prejudice reveals in startlingly regularity of adverse comments by senior male officers in their female colleagues' annual performance reports. If sexual advances by senior male colleagues were repulsed, there were chances of being shifted to undesirable posts. There were cases of molestation and sexual harassment.

The survey also cites discriminatory service rules. One such rule makes it mandatory for a woman officer to take government's permission before she gets married. Secondly, the physical standards requirements for height, and ability to walk distances etc. are tuned to the male physique.

Till 1st March 1954 women were excluded from the prestigious IAS & IFS services. The justification for exclusion was that women were unsuitable to serve in far-flung and remote places in the country and the world. These could be lonely and inconvenient for women. These services were the prerogative of males. In March 1954, it was decided to include women in these services. The IAS rule of 1954 was an obvious case of discrimination and went against the spirit of the Indian Constitution Rule 5(3) said, "No married woman shall be entitled as of right to be appointed to the Service and where a woman is appointed to the Service subsequently marries, the Central Government may, if the efficiency of the service requires, call upon her to resign". This highly discriminatory and controversial rule continued to exist till 1972 when it was deleted. But the positive decision to include her in the services proved a desirable impetus to the women's movements and education. The deletion of the clause of restricting married women in the services in 1972 further was an adjustment to the dynamics of women's role in the changing world. The political leaders observed that, women have something valuable to contribute to the society and country. It will be pity to lose that and close opportunities to them in this field of activity. It is hard to believe that 50 years back there was a long drawn battle whether women should be allowed in the Administrative Services.

Role of women in politics is the focused issue these days. "As long as the women of India do not take part in public life there can be no salvation for the country.... I would have no use for that Swaraj (local autonomy) to which some women have not made their full contribution"—Mahatma Gandhi 1925.

Seventy-three years later, women in India are still struggling to make effective contributions to the decision-making process, their voices are drowned in a cloud of male dissent. With only 36 women in the Parliament, and the 81st Amendment Bill (that aims at reserving a third of the seats in Parliament to women) has yet to take off, it may be quite a while before their struggle is over.

After over five decades of independence, just one perusal of the female infant mortality figures, the literacy rates and the employment opportunities for women are sufficient evidence that discrimination exists. This gender bias is evident in political system as well. Historically, the manifestoes of major political parties have always encouraged women's participation. It has been mainly a charade. Women opted for their last resort—the reservation of seats in the Parliament and in the overall political system; when they were denied place on merit. The political parties endorsed it initially counting on the vote bank of women. But this too was a mirage. In 1997, the then Prime Minister, I.K. Gujral could not place the Women's Reservation Bill in the parliament. In summer 1998 Parliament Session it is again being debated. This time the politicians are creating other dilemma. They want to include further reservation quota for women of backward castes and minorities. There is general apathy towards the bill among the politicians. Actually, it is a classic case of doublespeak: politicians were endorsing women's reservation in public but in the back rooms of Parliament they were busy sabotaging it. The reasons are clear. Men just do not want to vacate their seats of power.

Slated to usher in a new era of political participation for rural women, the 73rd and 74th Amendment Acts are reserving 33% seats in Panchayati Raj Institutions for women has not held much hope either. Most of these women are facing problems because of their lack of political education and prevalent patriarchal social attitudes. In northern India, a large number of rural women who are elected as local Panchayat government functionaries are illiterate and in Purdah. They are escorted by their husbands and family elders to Panchayat meetings and are hardly allowed to participate in the deliberations. Besides Purdah comes in the way of interaction with officials and functionaries. It is the male members who address the gatherings and take decisions. In some places even women are not brought to the Panchayat and their names are only kept on the records (Conference Feb. 1996 New Delhi).

An elected women representative complained that bureaucracy was preventing her from discharging her duties. "I promised people in my constituency money, water, and electricity but I have failed to keep my promise." Gang rape of elected women representatives, particularly those from the backward classes, reflects a violent backlash.

These are the kind of problems and challenges women have to watch out for and to combat with. Though women themselves are enthusiastic for participation. The first step consists in helping the women identify their more recurring problems. Second, is to increase their self-esteem and make them understand the power that they can wield, and the changes that they can bring about in the lives of other women. Third, the importance of bonding of women to work together and solve their own problems. The success story of getting women toilets in an industry (which they were deprived for many years though a basic necessity) by dint of their unity, is an example what women can achieve by a unified demand. Networking of government and non-government organizations and the mobilization of local resources are emphasized.

In India, currently in 90's women in politics face women-specific constraints. Such as maneuvering by their male counterparts, not able to mix easily with male colleagues for fear that people may misread their behaviour, misled by male political colleagues when ask for work related advice, criminalisation of politics, and husbands keeping a hand on political power through their wives. Dirty party politics, and manipulations often made women withdraw.

Pressures on women's income generating responsibilities have also undercut the time and energy that women can devote to organizing politically and socially. Political mobilization of women is essential to translate effectively women as policy constituency.

The findings of a research study (Women and Local Politics in Mumbai and London: the quota innovation, by All India Institute of Local Self Government Mumbai and East London Business School 1st part 1996) documents experiences of women corporaters and their difficulties as elected women from Sao Paulo, Sri Lanka, Bangladesh, Malaysia, Pakistan, and a few other developing countries. The study asserts that barring some cultural differences, all elected women face similar difficulties.

It further compares women politicians in London and Mumbai (India). In London, women politicians are more assertive, they do not let their husbands participate. They pushed for equal opportunity politics and raised such issues as social service, education, street safety etc. Both women politicians in London and Mumbai have initial reluctance to enter local politics, a lack of confidence and information but still women in India face more challenging task. In India, the most negative repercussion in political participation is the overwhelming influence of husbands restricting their participation, when husbands rule their wives constituencies by proxy, attending meetings, addressing redresses. This tantamount to men sheltering women as inferior, less capable and less intelligent. Recently even in 1997, in Bangalore, India, the males dominated the elected women municipal corporaters. But there were few dissenting voices to steal the thunder for fear that their marriages may be ruined.

Development and training programmes by political parties, government and autonomous institutes have to be an on-going long-term process if women are to climb the political ladder. All this depends on how our political parties are going to support women in the future.

They talk about and look forward to partnership of men and women in politics and to discuss about the strategies for making politics more inclusive to women. Women under-representation in politics is a strange anomaly because women in fact make up the majority of population and voters. Low rate of female representation in politics underlines true enormity of the problem. Such strategies focus on, reserved seats for women politicians in Parliament. Image of women politicians, and the media. Women's political and electoral training, and financing women electoral campaigns. The last one is of particular importance as women face serious financial barriers to political participation. Political power and role as a citizen are equally important for women. Most women view political participation as running for an elected position, but these are equally two important areas of political participation, One as a citizen and other as leader or a politician i.e. representative of the citizens. In the role as citizen lies the real political power in democracy (International Conference on Inter-parliamentary Conference New Delhi, Feb. 16, 1997).

Female Prime Ministers and ministers have ruled India, Canada, Sri Lanka, Bangla Desh, Guyana and some other countries. It is demonstrated that it is possible for women to rise to the top of political life. But each country's success shows that it is exception and not the rule.

Science and Technology Initiatives (STI) by women: Women in earlier decades of the 20th century had no exposure to science education and training. Women were users of conventional household technologies, farm technologies etc. They were essentially users of technology products and services. They were never contributors to technology promotion or innovators. The fourth generation was exposed to scientific education only in the early 50's. With the advancement of technology in varied fields; women were users as well contributors to technology. The fifth generation were exposed to rigorous scientific education and training in schools and universities. They are being exposed to advance technologies from global perspectives. Such a stance has created scientific ambience and opportunities. At present the STI scenario is that more and more urban and rural women from all strata of society are participating and have the potentiality to participate in STI applications, and in the affiliated infrastructure as Users, Contributors, and Innovators.

Women of today's generation are more aggressive and assertive. They push their way as strong, motivated, and powerful force in the above mentioned three ways: As Users of STI products, ideas, and services; they contribute significantly by diffusion of STI innovations and technology promotions through their need assessments, discontents, and demands. They use these ideas, products, and services to reduce drudgery of life, and improve quality of life, and protect environment. As users, they are in position to give feedback for more innovations and varied products in their priority areas, and for those fitting in their resources. These are significant for process of diffusion and technology promotion.

As Contributors in STI development by gainful employment or self-employment; they improve economy, their own economic, and social status. Women have contributed to STI innovations through fresh applications of mind, and innovations based on experiences with old technologies. They are innovators of STI ideas, products and services. Participation through these three roles enhances their economic, social, and intellectual status in society. It inculcates self-reliance and self-confidence for facilitating self-identity.

The moot question posed by current scenario of science, technology, and industrialization is: should we ignore or nurture the 50% strong work force of women population?

Low visibility of women on STI scenario does not commensurate with the amount of their participation, contribution, interest, and commitment to STI initiatives. Low visibility is due to gender role perceptions, and equal opportunities denied for work, wages, and technology promotion. Women do face visible and hidden professional, social and family constraints for pursuing STI initiatives.

To dispel the 'invisibility syndrome', the focus should be to create equal opportunities for them in these areas. It is imperative that women oriented diversity training, and personnel policies should be implemented. It is also important to sensitize men to the problems women face in society to develop STI initiatives as contributors and innovators.

It is crucial that women have access to jobs in industries but also training in technology. Therefore, the policy-makers must enact laws and policies to guarantee equal opportunities, technical education, and training for women. Women should be equally represented as trainers and participants in training courses.

The choices of roles and values that women have in this generation in the background of barriers that they suffered generations back such as gender stereotypes and limitations; encourages women to be more visible on the STI scene. Indian women have also gained through the global progress in STI. They are visible in high technical jobs as engineers, scientists, doctors, and technicians. They also get into middle level and lower level jobs in these areas. Women have also been sharing the affiliated infrastructure of science and technology applications by industrial planning, business plans and decision-making, administration, and diffusing STI at all levels of society. Women are visible both as self-employed entrepreneur, employed entrepreneur, business managers etc. both on national and international scene.

Indian women still face many barriers. The worldwide progress in STI over the last decades has not brought proportional gains for them. Enhancing women participation is not only necessary for doing social justice, but for reducing poverty, and improving their economic position.

Thus promoting women in STI is one point but to keep them professionally satisfied is another point. It is disincentive when their merits are not recognized. Women have stormed male strongholds. The male management is also learning that women diverse work force contributes diverse ideas and efforts in STI competitive world. But there are a very few women in elite and fast track line in STI.

The low skills, the low productivity, low wages, low access to education, and training in science and technology, and ungainful environment reinforce one another to keep women from STI development. Thus scientific temper and environment is not cultivated for them. The relevance and importance of technologies for women is not highlighted. Consequently women remain ignored factor in technological development. The fact is that women are ignored, and that they lack awareness, knowledge about opportunities and technologies. Therefore, they have little say in sensitizing the planners and functionaries to their economic, and technological needs and participation.

There is need to develop awareness, initiative, and push for creating more visibility of women on the STI scenario by three components: teaching, training, and technology promotion on equal footing.

Concern for Sexual Harassment. The Inter-parliamentary Union (IPU) suggests to take effective steps against criminal exploitation of women; such as the threat of rape as instrument of terror, forced prostitution, and all other forms of sexual aggression in armed conflicts. It condemns it. It further suggested that parliaments and governments adopt a programme, setting out standards for the protection of women and children in the zones of national and international conflicts. They should enforce appropriate measures to protect them from violence, eliminate sexual harassment; and to provide adequate support services staffed by women for the victims. Family violence needs to be prevented; services to intervene in situations of violence should be set up. They further recommended that UN extend the power of the international tribunal to ensure that States and individuals were held accountable for such crimes (IPU Conference, Feb. 1996).

Statistics show that the crimes against women are increasing with the advent of modernization and materialism. Women do face the humiliation of sexual harassment in public (even in public transportation), educational institutions, and work places. It is not the enforcement of law that is necessary but rather social awareness, change in social attitudes and accountability.

Sometimes, the temptation of luxuries for herself and the family, and her sacrifices to fulfil little dreams of the family overtakes a woman's morality. The call girl rackets operate in posh residential localities. The innocent educated young girls from decent families are drawn into this racket with the temptation of easy money. Her conscience is at eternal crisis. She is distraught with guilt (more so if she is married—the extramarital affair). She is unable to share her predicament with her parents or husband—try as she would. She trusts in marriage relationship, and her family relationships. But once in this racket, she is blackmailed further. Recently, police and women NGO have taken steps to protect women against call-girl rackets. But along with that social awareness and discipline is needed.

Crime against Women: The alarming increase in the rape cases: about 32% between 1990 and 1997 has not aroused concerns about condition of women in India. Recent (1998) Gang rapes in the university campuses were not only scandalous but also shameful was that it had political involvement. The statistics released by Pune based Association for Women's Studies (1998) revealed that one woman is raped every 54 minutes, that one woman is killed for dowry every 102 minutes; and 10,000 girl fetuses are denied life every year.

The battle to seek justice is however long and arduous one and lacunae in the laws always help the perpetrators to get scott free. Although a sustained campaign by women's groups has led to some amendments in the rape laws; but activists claim these are not enough. Abused women face legal apathy and social humiliation. Even as we reach the end of the millennium, the soaring graph of crimes against women shows no downtrend. Activists claim that though increasing trend is worrisome; it is also an indication of the fact that more such cases are being reported—that women have broken the silence and demanding justice for crimes perpetrated against them.

The disturbing social phenomenon is the insensitivity of judicial system towards women who come to court in situations of violence. According to a study by Sakshi (NGO), 'Gender and Judges: A Judicial Point of View' Delhi 1998. It surveyed 109 judges across the country. Interestingly, 76% felt the legal definition of rape was sufficient. 68% felt 'provocative' clothes of women were an invitation for sexual assault; while 55% felt moral character of a woman is relevant in sexual assault case.

The National Commission for Women (NCW) and other women organizations have demanded sustained, long-term awareness generation programmes specifically directed towards bringing about changes in the social mind set, for the removal of gender bias and creating a positive image of women. The psychiatrists feel that the rising crimes against women are a reflection of the deterioration of social values. They pointed out that even as women assert their rights, they are becoming targets of their attack, from men who felt threatened by successful women. By sexually abusing someone, they are trying to address their own insecurities. Activists point out that women would continue to suffer in one form or the other at home or in public unless men changed their ways of looking at women only as sexual objects meant for pleasure.

Activists and organizations have demanded that government not only initiate awareness programmes but also take active role in rehabilitating victims to overcome trauma they undergo, with special attention to their mental health. Unless law enforcement is made more stringent women will continue to feel threatened. Though laws are important in a civil society, they cannot fundamentally alter the status of the women. Violence against women whether domestic or social will be curbed only when the societal perception of women is changed.

As You Grow Old: The older women think sixty plus age as the time a world of individual roles and modes of personal behaviour can be chosen freely. It is the ongoing decade that gives the women chance to get out not only from a job but from much else that they have been doing unquestioningly for a long time. There is unsentimental wisdom about women growing old. The woman in her sixties gets the time for doing what she loves, for solicitude, she gets the pleasure of experiencing things which may be for last time. She gets friendships with other women, which are not recycling but full of discoveries.

Heilbrun Carolyn (1997) gives us vivid peep into what growing up old is coming to. The older needs relationships with the young or younger. But to have those relationships one must listen more than talk. They may count you as a tedious bore or just recounting the old anecdotes as a tape recorder. Does the older women still wants the marriage she has. She may be too frozen by fear, by convention, by what her children would think, to contemplate leaving a long established relationship. But when she is old she accepts her husband as he is who may never change; delights in conversations with her adult children who may think her ancient. But by this time she is honest, unsentimental, intelligent, wise, and relevant because she has thrown the doors open, let the light and air come in and experienced the long years of life with its ups and downs. Though old age is still a musty room rarely written about well. It gives a feeling of door in.

Generations' Images: The generation gaps i.e. the change among the generations overtime presents sociological issues. Times change and we as human beings change with the times.

The images of generations of early 1900 may be quite different and present a different worldview. In those days the positive image of a woman was that of a homemaker, subdued to the decision-making, wills and whims of men. A woman's confines were home and hearth. Her other preoccupation could be religion practiced within the confines of the home. The predominant image was that of weak willed women to be protected by men; delicate and beautiful physically and pampered by men by gifts of jewelry and clothes. Women were sex objects for procreation. Negative image was projected when women rebelled against the well-established system of gender discriminations within the families and societies. When women were treated as sex objects for prostitution and exploited by men to downgrade them in society.

The image of women in 60's, that is, in the middle of the century was one of struggling against discriminations and gender bias. An image of being actively promoted by social activists to gain access to education, career, marriage choices and freedom, economic independence and empowerment and a social and political voice of her own. Interestingly all this was the outcome of the restlessness of the women of earlier generations who were eager to come out of their shells. Luckily they were encouraged by their male counterparts who themselves were getting restless in not giving the rightful human rights and growth opportunities to the women that mattered in their lives.

The images of women in 80's and 90's were drastically different from the earlier generations. They had the advantage of changing global environments, the technological advancements giving access to variety of positive and negative cultural influences and at the same time opening a wide variety of opportunities. At home they had the advantage of growth, restlessness, and struggle of three generations of women trying to create an identity for themselves. Over and above, the national and international efforts focused on giving better lives to women *per se*.

A status report suggests that young females as a population is stepping out of many traditional stereotypes that have defined girls for generations. Some of the progress made is the result of public policies and private efforts to enhance the status. More subtle social pressure also had the effect of pushing girls.

Communication Forms, Issues and Women

Many women's participatory communication begins with fundamental part of her life-experience of being a girl child, growing environment for adulthood, experiencing motherhood, domestic work, and impact of domestic and social violence etc. These affirm or challenge the unique self-identity of women.

Variables		**Modes**		**Issues**
• Gender bias history • Cultural values • Empowerment	↔	• Communication expression • Communication access	↔	• Facilitating self-identity • Communication strategy • For projecting positive image

Fig. 2.2: Communication Issues for Women.

The complex variables of gender, culture, history, power intersect and shape women's communication experiences. They pose challenges to women's concept of self- and gender-identity, and to the process of negotiating and re-negotiating an appropriate balance between the experiences and revelations of their unique selves and their communication experiences as women in development process. Women's own unique and intimate experiences affirm or challenge the unique self-identity of women.

Communication about ourselves (women) can be two tiered, (a) revelation of hidden characteristics, (b) re-analysis of balance between what is unique to us as a woman and what is common in our experience as human beings. In communication, women may shift from presenting their concrete realities to expressing their ideal selves i.e. 'selves' they aspired to be—their enhanced visions. This suggests the importance of self-aspirations.

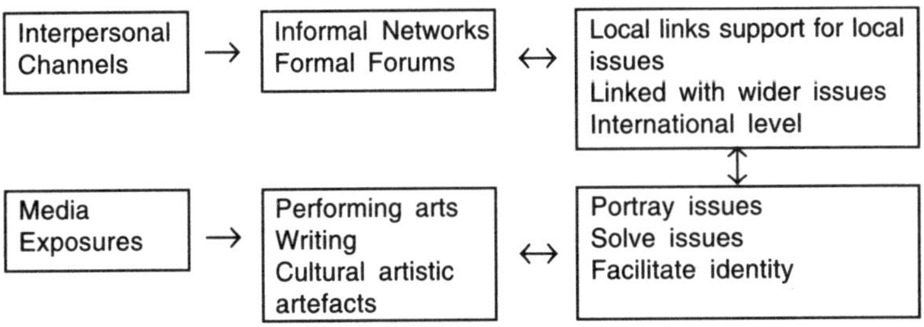

Fig. 2.3: Women: Communication Channels and Issues.

Women express themselves through channels of Interpersonal communication, of informal communication practices, networks and neighbourhood associations; and the formal group interpersonal forums. They communicate through performing arts, writing, cultural, and artistic artefacts etc.

These days women are effectively using media technology to portray themselves, to solve their issues, such as to use it as tools against discrimination, for defense of women's rights, and as spaces to reach larger audience. For instance, they may use the video, the broadcasting technology to express various aspects of their lives as well different perspectives of social movements. Therefore, they do become effective tools to provoke change. The attempt is to build feminine identity through media exposure.

A variety of communication means explore social resources, gender roles, economic distribution, and changes in tradition etc. with regard to women.

The important contribution of women's informal or formal networking is in its capacity to support local struggles by linking them with wider issues of regional, national, or international issues. Today, the technology such as teleconferencing and fax interconnect these individuals and groups through time and space; and to share experiences and concerns through process of personal and collective empowerment and power solving.

Through networks women can build their own bridges, share knowledge and concerns, develop research and communication strategies to recreate positive images of themselves. A communication strategy provides adequate structures and communication channels to empower women's knowledge and diffuse information and research.

Women's communication competence relates to three realms: indigenous knowledge, oral traditions, informal communication practices and networks. The social roles that women perform in their communities constitute the contexts that articulate these realms.

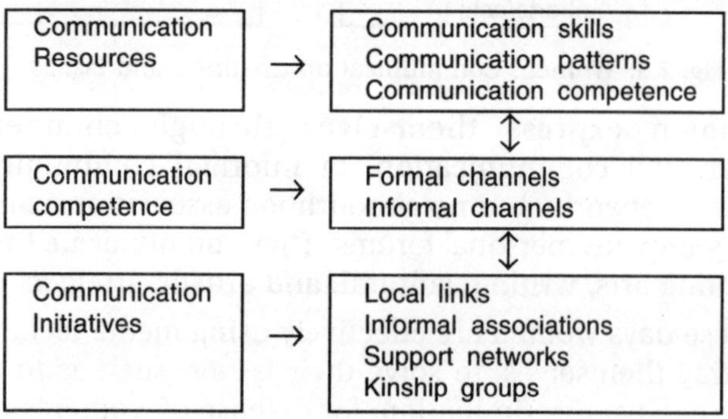

Fig. 2.4: Communication Forms: Projecting Women Images.

Women's personal and family experiences and the collective experience of group process constitute a socio-cultural resource base of communication skills, indigenous knowledge, and communication patterns and competencies. Their professional environments and experiences constitute a professional resource for communication skills, patterns, and competencies in work environments.

The assumption that learning empowerment process are exogenous to social community realm and are the direct result of outside interventions is not correct. This view disregards the vitality of women's communication roles and activities; interpersonal and social communication levels; through which women develop a concept of self and identity. Further, communication competencies are grounded in daily interactions that women as consumers establish with mass mediated products and services.

Women take varieties of communication initiatives such as local self-help groups, informal associations and support networks. Women in third world countries form and organize local groups, neighbourhoods in-groups to demand services and promote networks of survival and mutual help; and local social contexts for oral and feminine expressiveness. The local and neighbourhood groups are powerful informal networks to do information distribution, communication exchange that bind them for economic, social and political implications. Kinship networks are important systems of linkage among communication and lineage groups.

Analysis of communication experience from the perspective of social movements and multifaceted demands of everyday life concerns with access to basic facilities of life, improvement of quality of life for the self and family. They communicate as individuals, community, social, and public communicators. Issues of women's access to communication resources are linked to their social roles and community transformation; to women as socio-political and collective actors. The communication strategies are linked to their organizations and leadership roles.

Communication processes that have been used in women social movements focused on changing current critical practices, mobilizing the community for mass support, encouraging active support by creating public awareness among the women themselves and the community at large.

Based on data analysis of narratives of our sample Table 6.1 in Chapter 6 presents the communication patterns of expressing grievances by women over the generations.

Levels		Focus		Strategies
• Local • Family • National	↔	• Correct imbalances of gender bias • Create equal opportunities	↔	• Change attitude of man towards roles and responsibilities. • Laws • Accelerate socio-eco growth in specific areas of women life. • Encourage participation of women in socio-eco growth areas.

Fig. 2.5: National Strategies for Women Development.

Figure 2.5 addresses the national strategies for women development. Strategies are required to correct imbalances and discriminations. The improvement of the status of women requires action at national, local, and family levels. It also requires a change of men and women's attitudes towards their roles and responsibilities in society. Governments need to give firm commitments to, and high priority to legislative and other measures to accelerate the equal and full participation of women in economic and social development to eliminate inequalities between men and women in all sectors. They should identify areas to accelerate socio-economic growth of women and at the same time enhance the socio-economic participation of women.

Governments must ensure that advancement in technology has a positive impact on women socio-economic situation, working conditions, and health. That it provides women from the most disadvantaged sectors of population with the ways and means to increase access to infrastructure, basic services, and appropriate technology in order to alleviate the heavy workload imposed by demands of their families and communities.

Women need equality of opportunities in education, new skills development, jobs appropriate opportunities, and health care.

Women's needs and interests in their own development than those of the government's efforts can exert a demonstration effect to influence government policies. Role of women pressure groups in promoting women in development (WID) agenda is significant. There is a pattern of organizing women for protection against exploitation, for socio-occupational mobility through education and training, supportive services for children, and mother-child health care.

Four main patterns of political mobilization emerge when women make efforts to press their interests on the government through their local pressure groups. These are anti-colonial struggles, liberalization and democratization movements, traditional patterns, and emancipation through women's organizations. The government welfare agencies support women's traditional roles through income generating programmes. The pressure groups need to establish incentives and concrete programmes for increasing participation of women in decision-making process at all levels.

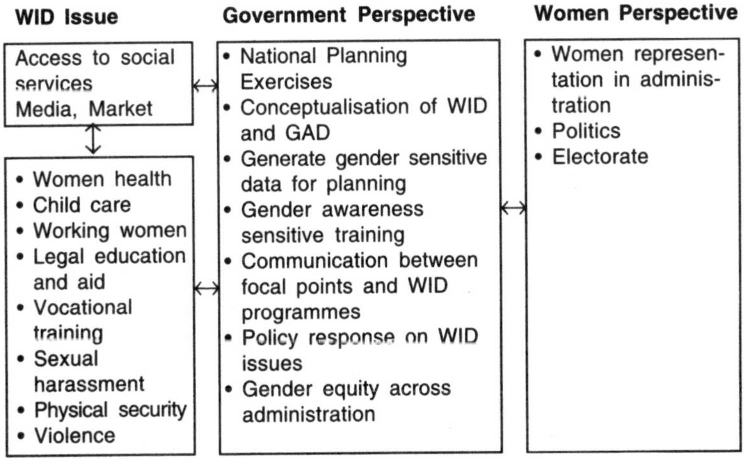

Fig. 2.6: Perspectives in Development (WID) Programmes.

There are a few implications for strategies to integrate gender issues to economic planning. One, stabilization and neo-liberal economic policies have gender-differential impacts on implications for women's time and income. Liberalization policies have provided formal and informal employment opportunities for women in combination with growing poverty in some contexts. Thus more women are moving into work force. But the unstable and transient nature of employment in informal sectors and in new forms may undermine any employment gains. This is shifting conventions around the gender division of labour, though not necessarily changing perceptions of women's work. These forms of employment tend to involve low skill, part time, and undervalued work.

Second, because of male resistance to gender-redistributive policies which imply 'zero-sum' trade off between resources for men and women, the equity-oriented policies promoting equal opportunities are acceptable only in times of plenty. Third, in periods of austerity governments are more sensitive and vulnerable to protest movements triggered by high rate of male unemployment. Fourth, weak administrative capacities in many of the developing countries may mitigate any gains, which are made at the policy levels in securing attention to gender specific concerns. Finally, the emphasis on neo-liberal economic policies, and to frame gender equity concerns in terms of social and economic efficiency gains will run a serious risk of losing gender justice and women empowerment.

Countries differ vastly in their degree of economic development. When it comes to institutionalizing women's interests in policy processes; no country is considered 'developed'. Problems faced everywhere are—profound bureaucratic resistance to the gender-equitable integration of women as subjects of public policy.

Historically, the injustices worked in women's lives by the power asymmetries attached to the gender differences across most social institutions have commanded a weak response from public authority everywhere. Typically, in all family welfare policies, women are shown as dependent on men. Women identity is equated to dependency on men. Thus the public policies are conditioned by such relationships. Even in efforts to integrate women in economic policy sectors, striking gender differentials persist in the design and implementation of the policy.

Policies for women tend to provide women with institutional survival bases—such as employment or asset ownership rights—which might be alternatives to dependence on men. At best such policies improve women's survival at the margins; at worst they can reinforce the traditional gender ideologies which contribute to women's disadvantaged position in their efforts to mobilize physical and human capital for self-development.

Focal point mechanisms have to be created to raise public awareness about gender issues, to challenge the acceptability of gender asymmetries in resource access and social values, and for promoting the development of women organizations.

In the WID process, the bureaucracy concerns itself with gender equity across administration, national planning exercises, the definition and production of gender-sensitive data for planning, alliance building with gender-aware constituencies within and outside of the government and changes overtime in the conceptualization of WID & GAD (gender awareness development) issues. Gender-awareness training provided to senior civil servants serve as a mechanism of communication between WID and focal points in ministries.

Policy responses are needed on one hand for such WID issues as working women's needs for hostel, child care centers, shelters for domestic violence, legal education and legal aid, vocational training, sexuality and sexual harassment in the workplace, and gender differences in the physical security. On the other hand, policies have to focus on conceptual clarity in identifying gender differences in labour deployment and resource control, women's access to markets, media, and social services. The formal WID units could be Advisory units, Policy monitoring units, and units with Implementation responsibilities.

Raising public awareness on these issues, legitimating them as matters for policy and planning; and thus amplifying women's 'voice' should be the responsibility of bureaucrats who are provided gender sensitive training and are in-charge of WID units. But some of the drawbacks are the gender paucity of senior women civil servants. More importantly, a few women who do gain access to administrative or political positions tend to be isolated from other women. They are under powerful pressures to conform to the dominant orientations of their institutions, the work patterns, and concerns of their male colleagues. These pressures limit their possibilities for developing sensitivity to, and acting in women's interests. Moreover, women's perspectives on public policy are more often rejected.

Obstacles to the increased representation of women at the senior bureaucratic levels are considerable the world over. They stem from structural problems from gender typing of women in the education system, labour markets, and from the competing demands of women's private lives. Women who do gain access to the bureaucracy get bumped into glass ceilings maintained by bureaucracy fraternity.

There have to be formal and informal mechanisms to enhance women's representation in administration, political and electoral participation from village to parliament, and representation in political decision-making forums. There is need to give importance and acceptance to women's perspectives on the public policies concerning their (women) issues.

The lack of awareness and commitment to gender issues among the junior personnel who handles the WID issues further puts the programmes on low key. Since only senior civil servants are trained in gender sensitivity training.

WID Agenda		**Efforts**		**Implications**
• Socio-occupational mobility • Protection against exploitation • Participation of women at all levels • Raise awareness about gender issues • Gender assymetries in resource access and social values	↔	• Local pressure groups • Political mobilization • National Govt. efforts • Women's own efforts	↔	• Bureaucratic resistance • Development strategies • Anti-colonial struggle • Liberalization democratic movements • Emancipation • Traditional Patterns

Fig. 2.7: Perspectives in WID Agenda.

The great variety of interpretations of WID depends on bureaucracies, political parties, religious institutions, women's organizations and non-government organizations (NGOs), and the international feminist community. In the international development community these concepts are subject to a spectrum of interpretations by donors. In some countries 'welfare' describes the WID policies.

In the new development inputs, credit, and technology are made available to women for the purpose of improving their traditional roles while at the same time servicing national concerns of family planning, population control, improved family nutrition and health care. None of these programmes opened women's access to non-traditional and sustainable employment opportunities.

Fundamental forms of social and economic restructuring over the decades, the appearance of new social movements organized on gender, democratization, and human rights grounds, and the growing conviction shown in the gender discourses of international donor community, have all contributed to the changes in the view of gender roles in the social sectors and in productive sectors.

Levels		Focus		Implications
• International development strategy • International conferences • International agreements • World media	↔	• Socio-economic reconstruction • Gender discourses • Women rights • Gender equity • Social movements on rights: gender, democratic, human	↔	• Global visibility of women • Exposure for intercomparison • International visibility and transparency of women abuses and injustice • Development strategies at indigenous level

Fig. 2.8: International Strategies for Women Development.

The international strategies for women development (Fig. 2.8) address the phenomenon of globalization as an effort for WID. The participation of individual countries in international conferences and agreements means that nations expose themselves for comparisons with other nations. Transparency at the international level means that abuses at the national level are more visible and more embarrassing to governments. Again, these can be exploited by women organizations to expose injustices and provoke responses.

So many governments over the world appear to be willing to commit to women's rights and gender equity in development process. Similar support is rarely given to class inequality. The reason has to do with politics. No government—bureaucracy has anything to fear from women.

The women all over the world are excluded from public political space, they lack histories of organizing on a corporate basis in defense of their own interests; although there are plenty of examples of women organizing along with men to pursue social, economic, and political agenda though not necessarily on their own terms. Even where women's interests do converge and find organizational expression, women often lack the financial and social resources, and political experience to make an effective impact on public decision-making. It is true that in some cases their non-conventional forms of protests such as against dowry, bride burning, price rise have impact on politics.

No women, gender trained researchers on the team, and male resistance to gender-awareness training can restrict the impact of gender desegregated data for WID.

Most of the development strategies of the past decades have excluded women at grass-roots levels from formulating, discussing, analyzing, or evaluating development programmes for themselves. Role of indigenous thinking in development programme is important.

Equality for women has become the password of our times. The UN while condemning the continuing violation of human rights and discrimination against women in certain countries also advocated financial equality of women. This is wonderful; but how much these lofty ideals are put into practice by many countries all over the world specially countries where bias against women is glaring. We look forward to the day when women's equality is no longer an issue to be talked about, to be taken up and fought for belligerently. A day to be reckon where women's equality becomes an accepted fact of life!

Woman 2000

Woman generations have gone through a journey of change. From demure and dependent to savvy and self-reliant, the personality of the woman has undergone a total transformation. Be it at home or at work, today's woman is in complete control of her life. With an attitude to match...she knows it all. She wants it all. Here is taking a look at the woman of the 90's. She is a homemaker; she is a career woman; is she a superwoman? What else do you call her? She does balance the multiple roles with aplomb.

With such demand on her time, little wonder that she could with all the help that she could get with all the new household gadgets—washing machines, washer-dryers, vacuum cleaners, dishwashers, microwave ovens etc.; computers with fax and e-mail at home and office, telephone with voice mail and answering machine. She is going in for anything that will allow her to have more time to herself and her family; and would afford more comforts, and more privacy to herself. 'Get empowered' seems to be her credo. With this realization, she is looking ahead; she sights new vistas, and new opportunities. With the kind of power she wields there is no stopping her—not till she is Woman of the World. That is why woman of the 90's will be a woman of the past. Woman 2000 sounds more like it.

The generation of 2000! How today's generations will live, work, and connect in the next millennium? What will be the face of tomorrow's teens? Who you will be in the next millennium?

Focus of the Book: This book is based on a empirical research study of women across generations dating back to 1900 to 2000 in Indian urban society, and those belonging to upper and middle socio-economic strata of the society. It is assumed that there is socio-cultural and development diversity among the women in these two layers of society; and they have experienced varied socio-cultural, and development changes which have molded their lives accordingly.

The plan is to study the lifestyles in general and inter-related development issues of women across five generations over a period dating back to a century (approximately 1900 to 2000). The study is based on personal anecdotes and analytical insights about women of five generations through composite perceptions of grandmother-mother-daughter relationships. The generation specific profiles of personal experiences of women talking to women from different generations are chronicled through their narratives.

This book is about building bridges across generations. At the most basic level, it concerns the bridges that individuals build in order to understand the events that they experience; and the bridges that connect the events in the mind's eye. These are manifested in the overlapping themes in their lives. People temporarily integrate individual 'snapshots' to form a coherent event that unfolds over time, to understand cause and effect, and to appreciate the role of the events. Another overlapping theme involves the possibility of individual differences within the generations. These themes are apparent in development of specific episodes, autobiographical memories, and comprehension of complex events involving multiple characters and emotions.

The book describes interesting narratives from three groups

of women from different generations. They talk about their own experiences and their perceptions about the other generations. The first group of women enjoying their eighty plus years narrate with enthusiasm how they perceive the generational change among their daughters and daughters-in-law. They are nostalgic about their own life, and even talk about their mothers and grandmothers. The second group of women in their sixty plus years talks about themselves, the lives of their mothers and mothers-in-law, and that of their parental grandmothers; and their perceived experiences of their daughters and daughters-in-law. The third group of younger generation women in age group of twenty years plus tells us about themselves, comparing, and reflecting on their mothers' and grandmothers' lifestyles.

The traditional accounts of women's lives have told stories of passivity that diminish or conceal the achievements and diversity to be found in their lives. The conventional approaches such as surveys, and close end interviews etc. to chronicle the lives of women have failed to capture the essence of feminine experiences. The narratives of our subjects are spontaneous, which highlight personal experiences, attitudes, ideological, and social forces operative at a particular point of time. These narratives reflect whatever were the turning points and of uppermost concern in our subjects lives. Their lives must be full of many more experiences and they may have much to say about themselves but limitations of our book could not write all that except the saliency of their life experiences.

Reality is gender neutral. Men and women have different responsibilities, needs and interests. These differences are not static but change through internal processes and external influences.

The empirical research study uses Qualitative Discourse Methodology, and Critical Incident interviewing. A quota purposive sample is selected to give depth to the study. Since the sample is small and not statistically representative of the large society; no generalizations are suggested.

The trend analysis presented is based on sixty oral and self reported narratives. These are spontaneous responses highlighting their own experiences, memories, reminisces, and flashbacks from their lives. These narratives are presented as such. No predetermined categories as focus of responses were suggested to the respondents. A few salient narratives from different generations are given in Chapter 7.

The sample of sixty narratives about women do not in any way represent large population of India. It is only a trend analysis—a situation analysis of change and development among women across generations in upper and middle strata of Indian Hindu society. But this surely does provide a glimpse of changing status of women in nineteenth and twentieth century.

The narratives are organized in three convenient groups. Group one includes narratives of women in 80 plus years; second group includes narratives of women in 60 plus years; and third group includes narratives of women over 20 plus years. All responses highlight how women have changed across five generations. The five generations are conveniently categorized for discussion and analysis as given in Table 1.

TABLE 1

Generation Categorization

Born before 1900	referred as grandmothers referred as mothers by 1st group 80 + age	1st generation 2nd generation
Born after 1900	1st group 80 + age	3rd generation
Born after 1900	2nd group 60 + age	4th generation
Born after 1900	3rd group 20 + age	5th generation

Analysis Focus

Narratives are analyzed on five-point analysis-schema. The generation perspective highlights the self-perception of women. The intergeneration connections highlight the other perceptions of women across generations. Transition point presents transition profiles of women across generations. Development point suggests the direction in which development efforts are geared across generations. The focus perspective suggests the major point of change. Every narrative reveals a very specific focus in the life of the narrator suggesting nobody live the same moments; yet all are connected to human life. The above analysis schema highlight the contributions women are making to the process of social change and the role that generational interconnections have played in activating them to such change.

Organization of the Book: How Readers will Enjoy Going Through the Book

The Prologue chapter reviews the way women have been perceived through generations, and discourses around women's issues in a particular societal context. The understanding of the particular societal context is necessary to know how they have evolved.

The generation thematic analysis is presented in Chapters 3 (3rd generation), 4 (4th generation), and 5 (5th generation). Every generation discusses how they perceived themselves and other four generations. The discussion is around eight categories describing the life styles and roles, gender bias, education and careers, marriage including divorce and widow status, health care, leisure activities, religion, and communication channels. The reader may find overlapping discussion about various generations around these categories. These are manifested in the overlapping themes in their lives and involve the possibility of individual differences within the generations. This may overwhelm him/her at times. The reader must organize focused reading to enjoy this book: Every thematic chapter will give the reader particular notions about how all five generations are perceived by the specific generation. The three thematic chapters will give him/her a sense of uniformity as well differentials in perceptions overtime. He/She will enjoy and appreciate these perceptions.

Chapter 6 concludes the study. A composite discussion on trend and situation analysis of all five generations around the same eight categories gives the reader a composite scenario of women development through the generations. Accordingly profiles of women of five generations are mapped in this chapter.

Salient narratives are reported in the Chapter 7. Reader will find this most interesting and will not like to miss it. The reader may get more insights through some of the subtle nuances in the narratives!

Reader is likely to note an interesting point in writing style when discussing about women—the change from third to first person or *vice versa*. This is deliberate to emphasis the point in discussion.

Enjoy reading Indian Women Across Generations.

3

WOMEN IN DIALOGUE: THIRD GENERATION WOMEN

We Women Talk: about ourselves, about others.

Group 1: Women in Eighty Plus Years.

Shackles, Shackles, Shackles
I want my freedom to grow.

Generation Perspective: Self-Perception

These women were born and were growing up as the 19th century was ushering in. They had the background environment handed over by their mothers and grandmothers who were the products of 18th century. The experiences retold by them highlight the self-perception of women in eighty plus years. The key points in their perception are: cloistered growth, denial of opportunities to grow as a normal human being, gender discrimination in all walks of life, and rigid social taboos. They suffered all this at the hands of their own fathers, brothers, and other close male relatives. But there were interesting turns of events for this generation as the Century progressed. Life changed for better for women and that too through the efforts of the males who have earlier denied them for whatever reasons. Let us hear what they narrate from their experiences. These are self-revealing.

Our analysis presents insights and challenges that the women faced in their times. The readers will find the self-reporting narratives given in Chapter 7 lucid, interesting, still more and more revealing, full of challenging anecdotes, and sometimes hard to believe.

Lifestyle: This generation of women grew up in sheltered lives; protected by males, and at the same time sheltered against male exploitation. This sheltered life denied women access to freedom of expression, human and legal rights, education, employment, and economic independence. So much so that even the innocent joys of outdoor leisure activities were denied to them as they were growing. These denials paved way for negligible social interactions, early marriages, bearing a large number of children, and suffering health problems and overall indignities as a human being.

The women lived dual and mixed lifestyles. Pre-marriage lifestyle was so different. It used to be a sheltered life, life of denial, stifled in four walls of the home. They faced gender discrimination at every walk of life even in such mundane matters as getting nutritious food. After child marriage at an early age, for some, life continued to be the same. But for others, life changed totally after marriage and they were able to develop themselves. Those who suffered after marriage did get respite by being cared by their children and grandchildren.

Women of this generation were leading two phased lives. The first phase, the early life and pre-marriage life up to fourteen or fifteen years of age was not eventful. It was a cloistered, sheltered life spent within the house. The second phase would start after marriage. This could be different as compared to the early life; depending upon who they marry. From this point of view, child or teen marriages might have been favoured. Since it gave opportunities to some of them to get away from the shackled life. Otherwise early marriages were not good for physical, and mental development of women.

The interesting point was that there used to be glaring gap in education among marriage partners. Since due to gender discrimination the males would be provided higher education whereas women learnt only 3 R's with no formal schooling. This stimulated males in the first instance to encourage women's education and inculcate respect for their (women) human rights. The males as they were growing up encouraged freedom of women among their marriage partners, female relatives, and daughters. They encouraged reforms about education, career, and marriage choices among them. They developed understanding about women's limitations in society, and stimulated women to develop and set their identities in life. Thus male activists played a significant role to give impetus to women development in that particular social setup. The male activists initiated 'movements' to free women from mental, physical and social exploitation.

Women's own aspirations for education, freedom, empowerment, independence; and the restlessness to achieve, encouraged the same traits among their own daughters and grand-daughters. Most of women in this generation are only literate. But they aspired for higher and professional education for their daughters, and also encouraged them to choose those careers that were earlier totally in male domain. The constraints in their marriages created better environment for freedom in marriage choices for their daughters.

Thus womanhood got boosted by urban values, male encouragement, not living in extended family, and also by their own efforts to some extent. Many felt that credit for women development during that period goes to British open society influence. British were ruling India during that period. Earlier, a very few women could participate in politics or social activist activities. But now many could volunteer for community services, and that is socially approved. The second phase of their life gave them independence, and empowerment.

Roles: There was bifurcation of male and female domains. Male dominated and handled outside matters and financial matters. Home, and specially kitchen was women's domain. Thus they had full say in taking care of the health and nutrition of the family. They were well respected and given status at home only. They neither had any say in the outside matters or any awareness, and knowledge was created among them about these matters.

Males of my generation, as they were growing up, aspired that married women should develop, have freedom of socializing with males, have access to outdoor recreation, and education. Some of them encouraged them to participate and get actively involved in planning for family activities. But women were scared and they were contented with only having 'a say' in household management. They considered management of the outside world as men's prerogative.

It was possible to play multiple roles in society as I had the advantage of education, career, and being social activist myself. But still I am convinced I could achieve these because of my parental sanctions in early life, and later an understanding husband contributed to it. But this was not true for most of them.

Those of my generation who enjoyed meaningful marriage relationships had no crisis of self-identity. Though these were few as there was conventional gender bias towards women's roles in life. Some how not many complained about these biases and accepted them as natural ways of life.

Overall my generation has hypocrite attitude towards life. They were denied many of their human rights yet they believed that is the way the life should be. In fact they made their daughters-in-law suffer the same indignities which they abhor for themselves.

Gender Discrimination: It was more pronounced in education, health care, and many socially tabooed areas for women such as gender mixing, going out unescorted, participating in outdoor sports, leisure and cultural activities such as music, dance and theater performances, pursuit of a career, choosing her own marriage partner etc. There was too much gender discrimination. They preferred to have sons—for financial as well emotional security in old age. As a choice, they would prefer to give their property to sons and grandsons, though legislation does provide for daughters' inheritance.

Education: Some of the women achieved higher education in spite of social constraints and repression. There was no social sanction to send women to school or provide education to them. Most of them did not have any formal schooling. But they enjoyed studying at home. At times male folks did encourage them to study at home in unstructured ways. But there was definitely gender discriminations in this regard. Males enjoyed formal schooling and higher education. Since it was felt that money should be invested in educating them as they were the income earners; whereas women were not going to earn. Nobody thought about educating them for developing their minds. There was gender discrimination. Girls were not sent to schools. In fact, there were no girls schools.

But girls were encouraged to learn the 3 R's at home only. In fact earlier generation of my mother and grandmother even did not have that opportunity.

Health Care: The public health care system for women was just developing. There were less of diagnostic, preventive, and curative facilities available. But still efforts were made to procure medical facilities for serious illnesses. Women mainly used indigenous home made herbal medicines for common illnesses. There was awareness about food nutrition for health. Women made efforts to provide the same to the family.

My generation suffered health care more because qualified female medical doctors were not available. Treatment by male doctors was tabooed. There were not many public hospitals to treat women. So many died without being treated. Health of women suffered from many pregnancies, and malnutrition.

Until 50's there were no family planning methods that women could use to limit and space their families. Even till 70's they could access them only with the consent of their husbands (so much for male domination and dependency). By 80's women achieved more independence of self-decisions. They did not need consent of their husbands for using family planning methods or for abortion even.

A large number of children in a family were preferred to inculcate good family relationships and family integrity. But small families through use of family planning devices became necessary to avert population explosion in the country. More population meant lots of hardship for the coming generations.

Marriage: Elders in the family arranged matchmaking. Girls and boys had no say in their mate selection. Mutual social and family status used to be one of the main considerations. Caste, community, and regional restrictions were very rigid in arranging marriages. Even the groom-to-be had no say about the physical beauty, mental or intellectual development of the bride-to-be. There were never any dowry-demands. The family would give minimal amount of clothes and jewelry according to family status as dowry.

Women never had sense of belongingness to the parental family due to early marriages. Mothers-in-law expected daughters-in-law to be confined to home. They restricted them to share husbands' work, social life, and pursuits. Thus they were restricted to have meaningful marriage relationships. But husbands encouraged the wives to develop even though mothers-in-law would be hostile (may be the 1st & 2nd generations could not get over their own restrictive life). Women grew up learning better household management. Divorce was unheard of. The wife will live with the husband, however, unhappy she may be as she had no independent status of her own in the society. She was dependent on her husband both financially and emotionally. Her parents would not encourage her to live with them. So she had to resign herself to fate.

Status of Widows: The widows could independently manage home and raise children as the late husband would mostly financially provide for such event. Not many of the women were earning. But they did get social, and economic status as now the women had the legal rights to husband's property and money. Provident funds and family pensions were provided to them as life long social security. Male activists made consistent efforts to get widows—legal and family rights. These efforts assigned better social status for women in the long run. Young widows without children were encouraged to remarry. Elderly women with children would not marry on their own. They were looked down upon if they married.

Religion: Religion and religious practices were only daily routines. Religion was exclusive domain of women within the house. Men seldom practiced religion daily except on festivals and rituals; where they assumed dominant role.

Leisure Activities: Women had less opportunities to participate in outdoor leisure activities whether sports or cultural. They enjoyed merry making during religious festivals and rituals. They could enjoy these activities only among women groups. This was also a useful way to throw social inhibitions though only temporarily. There was social taboo to intermix for entertainment with males and more so with unrelated males.

Communication Channels: In the first phase of life interpersonal communication channel was mainly used to communicate among family, friends, and relatives. In the second phase, their communication area expanded to friendship networks. Postal system was widely available, though telephone in urban areas was just coming up. Media technology was making progress. Radio, newspapers, and magazines were accessible. Media technology progressed a lot in the third phase of their life. They have access to radio, transistors, television, video and audiocassette recorders, and more facilities of telecommunication. This provided entertainment and leisure at home. They had better connectivity with the world even while sitting at home.

Inter-Generation Connections: Other-Perception

How did the women of third generation perceived their two earlier generations of mothers and grandmothers (1st and 2nd generations)? They also perceived the growth of their daughters and grand-daughters (who belonged to fourth and fifth generations). The third generation women were the only one who could personally feel the environment in which their mothers and grandmothers had grown. Equally, they could observe the growth of their own daughters and grand-daughters. Their observations develop interesting inter-generation connections among women across generations—the first to fifth generations. These observations are significant in mapping the process of change in women development.

In the following analysis you may not find them talking about all areas. They mainly projected which emotionally appealed to them uppermost.

Perceptions about 1st and 2nd Generations

Lifestyle: Mothers and grandmothers of the eighty plus women of today had very different lifestyles which in turn did affect the early lifestyles of these women. Those older generations led sheltered lives.

Men in these two generations (grandfather and father) respected women, gave them homes to rule without any financial worries. They were the providers, decision-makers about how to handle matters in life. But they were never concerned about developing the women *per se* in their life. They felt that women were contented to be at home, and produce children. Those men never thought that women did aspire to lead a different kind of life. Women appeared contented to them with their lot.

Generations earlier than mine suffered many indignities of life in the name of religious practices. These were made by men to have dominant role in society. Women had no freedom of expression. They had little chances to grow fully their human potentialities due to conventional gender restrictions in almost all spheres of life.

The older generations of women had almost negligible opportunities for education, careers. They had no outdoor or geographic mobility. The social and legal sanctions restricted the opportunities to be aware, be knowledgeable of their rights as human beings and as member of any society.

Gender Discrimination: Girls could not be educated due to gender bias, lack of female teachers, Purdah system, and gender segregation. The day-to-day male contacts were only with relatives, domestic servants, priests, and vendors who would come to the house to sell goods. Servants and vendors had to be older people. They would be in Purdah for rest of the males. To be born female was considered curse and female infanticide was quite rampant in those days.

Health Care: Both preventive and curative medical treatment was not accessible to them for serious ailments due to lack of medical facilities. Male doctors could not treat them due to Purdah; and there was lack of female doctors. On their own they took good care of their bodies by consuming nutritious food. They used indigenous herbal medicines for their ailments that were quite effective. The important point was that they observed utmost cleanliness in their lifestyles. May it be food, cooking, bath, clothes etc. The cleanliness was given religious connotations.

Marriage: Girls were married in childhood or in their teens. They had to observe Purdah. This was done mainly because of fear of sexual exploitation by Muslim invaders and Indian Royalty. Marriages were totally arranged by the elders in the family. Mutual social and family status used to be one of the main considerations. Caste, community, and regional restrictions were very rigid in arranging marriages. Even the groom-to-be had no say about the physical beauty, mental or intellectual development of the bride-to-be. There were never dowry demands. The family would give minimal amount of clothes and jewelry according to family status as dowry.

Due to early childhood or teen marriages, the girls' growth was influenced by in-law's position in the society and their values. They used to be married to far off places away from their own family, in a new village or town. Those days transportation was difficult. There were no planes, no trains, but only horse or bullock drawn carriages, boats, or walking on foot were the major modes of transportation. There were no postal system, or telephones to keep in touch with the family. Girls could hardly visit the family and sometimes never in their lifetime. It was said, 'girl on marriage would leave her parental home in Doli (men carried carriage) and never come back. Only her dead body will leave from in-laws home'.

Divorce was never practiced. Wives were seldom abandoned. If condemned for one reason or the other; they continued living in the family till they died. Even as such as a married woman, she had no independent status in the household. Therefore, as abandoned wife she had more or less the same living status.

Widow Status: However rich they may be when they become widows, they would be at the mercy of their male relatives who would control money and family decision-making. But the good point was that if widow was left penniless; her relatives would provide for her and her children. Whether she was provided comfortable life or not was beside the point. But she was not allowed to remarry however young she might be. That was sometimes very cruel. She had no social or economic status. A widow was always treated as an ill omen by the society. She was not allowed to participate or even touch offerings in any religious functions or marriages etc. She was denied good living, good clothes, and even good food. The reasoning behind it was that an austere life would curb her sexual desires!

Religion: Women would say their morning prayers as a routine activity. They would spend most of their spare time in reading or listening to holy religious books and scriptures. It was a kind of leisure activity for them that diverted their minds from daily mundane routine of life. They practiced religious rituals at home. They were not able to visit temple frequently due to Purdah. With special arrangements women would visit temple on festival days. In fact, if the family was rich, they may have a small temple in the home premises for their family deity. But only priest would do daily puja (offerings) in the family temple; women were not allowed to do so. Women could do puja in their private chambers only.

Communication Channels: Women had only interpersonal communication within the family. They had to observe Purdah from unrelated males. The male contact was with relatives, domestic servants, priests and vendors who would come to the house to sell goods. Servants and vendors had to be older people. Women could not even develop or enjoy friendship networks. Television, and radio had not reached the media scene in India. A few newspapers were being published; but then not many women were able to read them. Even these were not accessible to them. Theater, folk music, and dance performances were popular means of entertainment, and educational messages. Women had no access to them as these were outdoor entertainment. Silent movie era has just started. But cinema was not easily accessible to all people at all places; and definitely not accessible to women.

Perceptions about 4th Generation

Lifestyle & Roles: My daughters' generation (4th generation) has been moving ahead. They were achieving, but in a more relaxed way as compared to the women of today (the fifth generation). They too fulfilled the twin roles of homemaker and that of career women. They also faced the new challenges of social change, for career choices, for marriage choices and the resultant legal implications. In this process they tried to establish an identity of their own. Marriage is a meaningful relationship to them. They share the life roles with their husbands of being decision-maker, home manager, and provider for the family.

As compared to me, they were better placed for education, professional choices (mainly in female dominated areas), and marriage choices. They gained from parental experiences, media exposure, and travel. They faced comparatively less gender discrimination in these areas. Women were not cloistered but they were protected against any kind of sexual harassment. They extended their social contacts with the outside family groups though they remained close knitted to own family groups. They remained quite conventional in their family and social value in spite of outside social influences. They are confident to face the life issues and solve them; and struggle independently in the process. They did suffer the ill effects of domestic and social violence that was on the increase due to variety of reasons.

Health Care: Physical fitness consciousness and participation in many outdoor sports and fitness programmes are new and healthy trends. These trends created better health status for them. Both preventive and curative health care improved with advancement in medical technologies and researches, and by availability of female medical doctors and paramedics. Health awareness and knowledge also improved due to education and media reach.

Marriages were facilitated. Women had a say in the selection of mate though parents would select the person initially. Mainly women did not have wider opportunities to meet the right kind of person to select for marriage. Divorce legislation has been introduced. The rate of divorce was very low since there was low social sanction for divorce. Divorcees have low social status and almost negligible chances of remarriage. Widow remarriages are not objected but not encouraged socially. But they had social, economic status and could live with dignity within the family—parental or in-laws. Living on her own was looked down.

Religion is confined to observing religious rituals and festivals. Temple visits are occasional. They do practice good values of life.

Communication Channels: The advancement in media technologies and in the expansion of interpersonal channels such as variety of networks and forums created connectivity, entertainment, and leisure both at home and in the outside world.

Perceptions about 5th Generation

Lifestyle & Roles: The younger generation of women of today (the fifth generation) are more stressed out because of competition, demanding multiple roles, and aspirations for perfection and efficiency. No doubt they have achieved more than any other generations. But the men of today are not tolerant of educational or intellectual gaps among their life partners. They look for matching personality and intellectual traits. In fact they physically, psychologically, and emotionally torment women and exploit them socially in the name of equal gender participation.

They are achievers. Quality of life is better for them as compared to other generations. But life is very competitive, demanding, and stressful. They consider it challenging and seem to enjoy it; whereas the older people think it is unmanageable. Demanding and competitive roles create physical and emotional stress. Over and above she lacks the supportive services of family as she does not live in extended family by choice or compulsion.

My grand-daughter's generation is so different in their values, lifestyles, and ways of life. They are not at all conventional. These women are self-centred in pursuit of their own identity—a multiple-identity. They interact less with kith and kin of the extended family. Rather they spend more time in sharing life with husband and children. They bring up their children differently. Children are brought to be more independent, more creative, interactive with diversified group of people, and exposed to variety of media channels. They spend lot of time in elderly care. They provide for care if they cannot take care themselves. These women work outside their homes. They do have a balanced perspective of life as compared to earlier generations. They enjoy multiple roles, challenges, and tensions of life. This generation has more social, and economic empowerment, and political awareness.

The upcoming younger generations have moral dilemmas because they are low on human values. But they are not hypocrites in their ways of life as mine or earlier generations were. Younger generation is better equipped to face the multiple challenges of life in their varied roles since they have wider opportunities for education, careers, and better marriage choices. The exposure to global ways of life through variety of channels provides them advance information and knowledge. They have social sanctions to practice what they believe. Moreover, there is 'Political Will' to develop women as nation's asset. They are not to be treated as unproductive and uneconomic segment of society.

Career: They choose career orientations according to choices and interests and not as compelled by society or parental choices as were done in earlier generations. The emphasis is on individuality through social and professional interactions. Working outside the home has essentially given women confidence to handle life. Moreover, these days women are protected a lot by legislation such as inheritance of property and money, dowry, divorce, marriage, employment, equal wages, maternity leave etc. It was necessary to do so since things have taken an ugly shape. In government, and in private sector there is no discrimination for employing qualified women. But there is discrimination in giving equal wages to women in private sector. Gender discrimination is also subtle in some areas such as to pursue certain careers, and avenues for promotion at higher levels.

Health Care: Women were healthier earlier as compared to the present younger generations; though there is lot of advancements in medical technologies these days. My daughter's and other coming generations are promoting small family norms by having one or two children only. They are aware of the overpopulation consequences. They support small family norms for self-health, quality of life, and for national cause of limiting overpopulation. But begetting one or two children only can always cause anxiety. What would happen if one of the children dies, has stunted physical or mental growth, or he is failure in life?

Marriage: Women marry of their own choice and sometimes they are facilitated also. Caste, creed or community restrictions for marriages are no longer that rigid. Whatever it may be, they have less time to nurture husband-wife relationships. There is higher rate of divorce among 5th generation. On the one hand, the personal factors responsible for divorce are the marital discord, mutual incompatibility, and mutual intolerance. On the other hand, the social factors such as the increasing domestic violence, and dowry demands due to material greed of the family goad it. The economic independence, efforts for self-identity among the women, and the confidence of the women to cope up with single parent homes further encourage it. Social and legal sanctions of the divorce make it more and more viable. Divorcees remarry. There is no social or legal taboo on widow remarriages at any age. Widows do remarry for emotional and financial security.

Generation Transition Period

The transition period reflects the changeover in the life of coexisting generations. This process of changeover is overlapping at times. The transition profiles give a comparative stance from across generations and reveal interesting trends.

Lifestyle: Women of earlier generations of 1900 were happy, contented, aspiring less, and helpless. The trend became downward for the first two traits for the coming generations till today. Aspiration trait was going up and up and the feeling of helplessness was replaced by a feeling of restlessness that grew along with the generations.

Life became more open and less sheltered. Protective life was gradually giving way to independent existence. Late marriages, family planning devices meant less reproductive years thus suggesting greater freedom for women. Less reproductive years and small families leave more time for women for other pursuits.

Women of today, especially younger generation enjoys quality of life, as well challenges of life. Life is becoming more demanding, competitive, and stressful for them. The society is undergoing change. It is becoming more open as far as women lives are concerned. Life is no longer cloistered and stifling. There is gradual but definite change in women's perspective to life across generations. They are more aware, knowledgeable, and very involved in solving life's issues. There is change over in ways of life and human values; the change is from conventional to modern.

As for social interactions, they no longer depend on interpersonal family contacts only. In fact they focus on wider social impersonal networks of both professional and social. Media exposures, travels and other extrovert outer activities create awareness and knowledge gain.

Marriage: The sanctity of marriage has changed overtime. Divorce has individual, social, and legal sanctions. There is higher rate of divorce among younger generations. The major factors responsible for it are marital discord, mutual intolerance, women's economic independence, and their efforts to establish their self-identity. On the other hand, the increasing domestic violence, and dowry demands due to material aspirations of the younger generations activate more divorces. The confidence of women to cope up with single parent homes further encourages it. Social and legal sanctions for the divorce make it more and more viable. The women have overtime achieved the right to choose their own mates with less caste and creed distinctions.

Gender preferences and biases are changing but still sons are preferred for the sake of old age emotional security rather than for financial security.

In short, the transition across the generation is towards a less hypocrite life for women, less gender bias in many areas. There is Social and Political Will to develop the potentialities of women as a nation's resource and thus create wider opportunities for them. The global influences in education, career, lifestyles, consumerism, and international business strategies have brought drastic changes in the younger generations of today. These have given them a confident image as compared to older generations. Advanced media technologies have further reinforced these possibilities. Environment for social sanctions and support is reinforced by legislation to protect women.

Communication Channels. This highlights the communication channels for interaction, information, knowledge etc. The research shows that both mass media and interpersonal communication channels have changed across generations in usage styles. The change occurred as the needs for interaction, information, and knowledge had undergone change. Further, advancement of technology did affect the mass media reach. The women had access to oral and interpersonal communication and relied on it. If literate, they read religious books and scriptures. Radio was a channel for political news in late 1930's. Traditional modes of communication such as religious gatherings, folk entertainment could be enjoyed occasionally only among women gatherings.

Social interaction whether casual or formal was only occasional for first and second generations. The social interactions for women changed overtime. They no longer depended on interpersonal family contacts only. In fact, they focused on wider social impersonal networks of both professional and social. Media exposures, travels and other extrovert outer activities created awareness and knowledge gain. The media technologies created more media channels. Some of them such as satellites created more global influences in various walks of life. Women were gainers to some extent.

Development Point

It pointed to the direction in which women development was geared on account of generation perspectives and intergeneration connections. It was felt that social structural changes, social and political activism, and legislation were needed to bring about the generation transition.

The social and legal sanctions for divorce are necessary for women development. But what is more important in today's Indian society is to create social ambience, and social movements to protest and fight against the social evils like dowry, and domestic violence. These are the major causes of divorce these days. Marriage and family stability are basic necessities for woman development and for her achievements.

Consistent efforts have been made to create wider opportunities for women for education, employment, health care, and to give her dignified lifestyle through development programmes as per national development policies. Social activism has further reinforced social reforms already legislated against conventional gender bias in all areas such as Sati (wife burning), inheritance, marital laws, and violence against women (such as bride burning due to dowry) etc.

There is Social and the Political Will in the nation to develop women by providing wider opportunities through legislation, and reinforcing them by social activism. There have been efforts to downplay gender bias and male domination.

The success stories of ongoing development of women, as well the indignities suffered by the past generations of women are impetus for coming generations to look forward and strive for a transformed lifestyle. Women are demanding their rights, protecting themselves, and in this process they are getting more assertive and more aggressive.

4

WOMEN IN DIALOGUE: FOURTH GENERATION WOMEN

Group 2: Sixty Plus Age Group

> *Eve teasing was the worst social crime against women that this generation suffered. It was very humiliating. An unescorted woman was looked down upon as sex object only. I remember when I had to come from my evening college classes. It will be dark and I had to take a long route to reach home to avoid a small deserted lane close to my home. Why? Some men would be just hiding there on cycles or otherwise to push me down, pull my veil, throw beetle juice on my dress, or touch me or talk dirty.*

Generation Perspective: Self-Perception

Lifestyle: This generation experienced the freedom to grow. It was the 'transition generation'—the first one since the start of the century to move towards modernity. They were given the freedom and opportunities to decide what they wanted to be in life. They looked forward to so many achievements; warm family relationships, professional education, career, marriage of own choice, social and political participation. Their dreams came true and they did achieve these to a greater extent. But they had to struggle hard to achieve in reality what was being offered to them. They were exposed to different channels of growth and were struggling as first timers for many things to achieve. Their achievements were initially the result of struggles, sacrifices, and even public ridicule. It was the first time that they were experiencing the openness of society for women.

'Male Domination Effect' stimulated women to achieve more. Women had explicitly and implicitly resented the domination. Aspirations of earlier generation of mothers were active stimulation for achievements of daughters. Enthusiasm, understanding, and education of parents motivated them further. Even if the spirit of some of the mothers (third generation) had been crushed by male domination still they had the lurking desire that their daughters should shape their own lives. Though in such families father and brother played encouraging role for younger women to grow. In general in the families, not only father, husband, brothers facilitated women to grow and were enthusiastic about the equality given to them. They respected this 'new woman'.

They had access to different disciplines of education, variety of jobs, professions, and careers. They had to struggle hard for freedom for expression, and for achieving self-identity. The good point was that these women had the parental support at home and support of the National Political Will. Their human rights for marriage, inheritance, equality in education, employment, and wages etc. were being protected by government legislation. She was asserting herself for her self-dignity, and in making decisions for herself. Various decades in the life of this generation were fast moving. They brought substantial changes in the women's life *per se*. Years from 1950 to 1970 were great for making efforts for women education and giving them legal protection in many spheres. New vistas were opening for women in professions, politics etc. in the years 1970 to 1980. The decades of 80's to date are more achievement oriented.

It was the first time that women were more visible in many spheres. They were more vocal about themselves and their rights. There were government and non-government efforts that focused on women development programmes *per se*. But this new image had some negative repercussions too. Crime against women such as domestic and social violence, eve teasing, rapes, and insecurity in moving unescorted increased.

Credit goes to British influence in India in early days for giving women a different kind of life. They banned Purdah, initiated girls' education, provided health care to women through trained medical doctors and paramedics (providing training and education in medicine), and thereby improving their quality of life. Later (after 1947), the national government gave social empowerment to women by legislation for inheritance, marriage freedom, divorce, widow and divorcee remarriages, anti-dowry and anti-Sati etc. They got economic empowerment through education, training, and skill learning, and through job openings. Fourth generation women benefited the most from the efforts of the national government. They also benefited from the international awareness and efforts to bring women to mainstream development since 1950's.

Life was more relaxed for my generation. We had discipline in life. We were allowed limited freedom to socialize with males. We respected those boundaries and never let down our parents. Life for women was not cloistered or over-sheltered like earlier three generations but still it was over-protective. The argument given was that over-protection was mainly for providing social security against crimes and sexual exploitation. Women were experiencing, that too much sheltered life by family males (as in earlier generations) was constraining social and professional growth of women. Moreover, they felt if they were not assertive, there were greater chances of getting exploited.

We shared life with family, husband, and children. Women were getting more empowerment in family life, decision-making, and financial management. Thereby they were gaining self-identity.

My generation had opportunities for higher education, and wider career choices. They had freedom of marriage choices. The caste and community restrictions had become less rigid for mate selection. Employment gave economic independence to women and that created self-confidence in them. They were enjoying wider and ever increasing opportunities for education, employment, careers, choices for marriage and raising family, better lifestyles and improved health care.

My generation had been exposed to global ways of life, technology, and modernization that stimulated them for achievements both in personal and professional areas. Their life is more technology oriented both at home and in work place. Modernity and post-modernity syndromes have affected the lifestyles of women such as marriage, divorce, health, small families, careers, and search for self-identity.

As usual, this generation experienced double lifestyles that were overlapping. In those days most of the women were experiencing a constraining lifestyle in their early childhood and pre-marriage, followed by more open lifestyle after marriage. Low restrictions in marriage choices, legal and social sanctions of divorce, remarriage, inheritance and economic independence had let women grow socially healthy and with self-esteem. Women have changed from non-assertive, subdued personalities to aggressive, self-centred, egoist, and opinionated women.

The typical feature of 4th generation lifestyle was the dilemma of 'woman making woman suffer'. On one hand the restlessness of 3rd generation made their daughters achieve what they missed in life. But on the other hand this generation of women (as mothers-in-law) deprived of own opportunities were jealous of daughters in-law achievements. They made them suffer through domestic and social violence such as physical beatings, mental tortures through demands of dowries, dowry-burning deaths, and even divorces.

Women development *per se* had given quality of life to them. Factors such as political participation of women themselves, and science and technology have contributed to women development. On the whole, women were growing in two parallel ways—open and constrained. They were putting up boldly with these ensuing conflicts. They developed hypocritical attitude towards life for fear of social disapproval. For social approval they were conventional in their dress and behaviour. Though they did suffer in the process.

Roles: Women of my generation got involved and delivered multiple roles in life effectively. Managing home, family, and career not only assigned different roles but a challenge for coordinating effectively her time and energy. They kept pace with changes in society in order to be more effective and create a visible position for themselves. Since they were moving out of home confines, they faced and experienced the external demands of society.

Initially, life was full of challenges and struggle for achievement. But they accepted them in order to be a generation with a difference. The challenges taught them to be open, straightforward and not hypocrite about life because of social disapproval.

They fit well in home management roles. They share life with husband and children and have more involvement with family decisions. Women did share life with husbands but had more protective attitude towards children. They imposed their will and choices on children particularly daughters. But this protective and zealous attitude stimulated children for higher achievements. On the whole they provided good upbringing to them. As a matter of fact women were raising large families as compared to 5th generation; though definitely smaller in size as compared to earlier three generations. The average norms of family size have changed through generations. Begetting six to twelve children was normal for first, second and third generations. The fourth generation restricted the size to three to four children, whereas fifth generation only wanted one or two children. The changing size of the family due to variety of reasons also created wider and changed vision of life for women of fourth generation.

Gender Discrimination: As generations progressed, one could feel less gender discrimination by parents in upbringing daughters. There were less gender biases for education, work, and marriage where parents were educated and enlightened. But still parents comparatively spent more money on sons' education; since it was considered an investment. In certain situations older brothers did not let their sisters work in male environments. Was it due to protective attitude or jealcusy for women to grow?

Otherwise women were still facing constraints on these issues from society. It was a period of gender segregation rather than discrimination biases. Women were allowed formal schooling and college education but there were schools and colleges exclusively for women. Only women teachers taught girls. Women were working alongside males, but they were segregated in work places such as seating arrangements, lounges, cafeteria etc. Women were assigned separate spaces in buses, cinema houses, and restaurants etc. Women felt segregation in work places where they had very little interaction with male colleagues. They were not allowed to stay back in office after office hours even if it was necessary to finish a piece of work. The reason being that she would not have protective environment after office hours as only very few employees might be staying back. Women felt it was not a good way to pursue careers. Does the whole idea of segregation was to protect them, show respect to them or a way to ignore them? Most probably the idea was to give protection to women, since women visibility and freedom of movement were new in the current social set up and somewhat hard to accept by many in the society. Parents too were giving sheltered life to women out of social compulsion. Mainly because of fear of social disapproval, women were not allowed freedom of outdoor movements. Protection of women in outdoor life became essential, as certain elements in society were still not ready to treat women freedom with dignity. Women were provided protected life for fear of sexual exploitation. They were protected by segregation of sexes at home, in work places, and in public places. Most of the men still considered her as sex object and did not respect her freedom. Though to a certain extent, the co-working in jobs have made men respect women freedom and create an environment with less fear of sexual harassment.

There were restrictions in gender social mixing. A woman could not mix socially without a male escort. Inter gender mixing without an escort was not approved. She could be labelled as woman with loose morals if she intermixed all by herself.

Education: Urban women were getting opportunities for education in general and professional education in particular. This was made possible by parental attitude, British government policies promoting compulsory education, and through the efforts of male social activists. The subject areas for education were still limited and there was gender bias in this regard. The educational opportunities were developing well aware and informed group of women, and training women in the professions of teaching, medicine, and paramedics. These professionals again in turn created opportunities for education, and health care for women.

Employment had given women freedom from male (in the family) oppression. Change in attitude towards working women had made women career oriented, productive, and seeking those professional fields that have been mainly in the male domain. The fourth generation had to struggle hard to make a niche for themselves in the male dominated professions; and to graduate to middle level positions. They were never assigned policy level higher positions. They were discriminated for promotions even.

In 50's more and more women had started working. They were the young work force. They were provided segregated and protective environment in the work places. Parental and work place discipline demanded that working women should observe subdued mannerism, behaviour, and conventional dress modes for fear of sexual exploitation (sic). However women felt constrained by such censorship, they abided by the restrictions. They did not want to loose their newly won freedom at any cost.

Majority of the women chose not to work after marriage. They preferred to devote time for raising family. Women employment was essentially associated with economic necessity. Later in life as they were growing old, and their children were getting settled in life; they felt the urge to work. To work was to get wider perspective on life, people, problems, and updates on society.

Health Care: Women had access to better health care on two counts. First, they were getting health conscious and aware of the need to take preventive as well curative measures. Second, the medical treatment was accessible to women now due to the availability of female doctors. They could not consult a male doctor due to social taboos; though these women were no longer in Purdah. They were getting conscious about maintaining good physique and well-groomed bodies. But visits to beauty parlours were occasional. There were no public fitness centers but the focus was on doing physical exercises at home.

Marriage: Women were demanding freedom to choose their own marital lifestyle; when to marry, and whom to marry. Women could not choose their own marriage partners. They were not restricted so much because of social constraints but mainly because they did not get the opportunities; as free gender mixing was not allowed. Parents were encouraging marriage choices through facilitation and arranged marriages. There was social disapproval for going steady. Parents were guided by social approval for match making. Women were not allowed to remain single. Caste, and community restrictions had become less rigid but still inter-religion marriages such as Hindu-Muslim, Hindu-Christian were socially disapproved.

This was the first time that national government protected the marital rights of women through divorce legislation. It was felt that right to divorce would protect women against domestic and social violence, and exploitation. Further, this would give women a chance to lead a humane life. Fourth generation felt this as an impetus to their development. Thus there were legal sanctions for divorce but still social support was not forthcoming. Those who were divorced, underwent traumatic life experiences due to its lengthy process and social complexities. They had no social status. Women had to struggle hard to gain the social status that younger (5th) generation of divorcee women have achieved today. Legally, divorcees could remarry. But there was low social support for divorcee remarriage. Remarriages as such had legal sanction but there was low social support for divorcee remarriages as compared to widow remarriages. Divorce was socially acceptable only in case of extreme hardship. A divorcee had to live under parental protection throughout her life and was not allowed to set up her own independent life. Legislation protected women against bigamy and polygamy.

Widow Status: Widows were accorded respectable social status and earlier social taboos were disapproved. They could dress, wear jewelry, participate socially in the normal way. Though some were still superstitious of widow in some situations. But they were no longer humiliated or had to bear the indignities of life. Widows would generally either lived with in-laws or parents; but they were not encouraged to set up an independent life. Widows had the right to their husband's property and money through legislation. The financial status gave her social status too. There were legal and social sanctions for widow remarriage. But remarriage of women with children was not socially acceptable.

Religion: Religious practices are a matter of one's own choice. There is no compulsion to observe them. Religion has been a way of life without compulsion of rituals. The focus is on God and good values of life. Women would observe religious festivals and rituals. They would participate in religious gatherings and discussions (Satsang). They would occasionally visit temples. But they were not compelled to follow any of these practices.

In earlier generations, religion was an important part of woman's life. It provided solace to them. It focused mind and was a healthy pastime. The many rituals and festivals did unwind the self when life became unbearable with so many constraints. Now the times have changed and so too the connotation of religion for women. Now women prefer to say prayers at home, and visit temples occasionally. They observe few selected rituals like wedding and a few religious festivals. They do not have to unwind themselves in anyway. Women today have philosophical and practical attitude towards religion. For them morality is person specific.

Leisure Activities: Gradually, learning and participation in music, dance, and theater was being socially accepted. Women would learn these and other fine arts. They would also spend time in learning household management, cooking, sewing and other related arts and crafts. In fact to help mothers in cooking, stitching, family entertainment, and looking after the younger siblings were also major pastimes for unmarried women. This gave them practical training in home management. Both fiction and non-fiction were read avidly. Socialization with women friends (within limits) was a favourite pastime.

Communication Channels: Interpersonal communication channels within the family and outside groups created a social network for awareness, information, and knowledge. Within the family these channels created cohesiveness. Being exposed to education helped them to use books and other print media to gain knowledge. This was the beginning of radio, audio-cassettes and recorders; and later television, video-cassettes and recorders completed the media scene. These technologies created better communication channels for women and also generated leisure time activities for them. Telephone density was low even in metro urban areas. Only in 70's it became an effective communication channel.

Technological advancement was good for women. It provided technology for better household gadgetry, for entertainment, and at work place. Women were exposed to global ways of doing, thinking, and knowing about diverse cultural ways of women in other parts of the world.

INTER-GENERATION CONNECTIONS: OTHER PERCEPTION

Perception of 1st & 2nd Generation

Lifestyle & Roles: My grandmother and great grandmother generation i.e. the second and third generations had to observe Purdah, and they had to remain within the confines of the home all the time. They had no outside social interaction far less male interaction. There were separate women and men quarters for living arrangements. Men use to come to women's quarters sometimes for food or for sleeping with their wives. Living in extended family was a boon those days for women since men would spent most of their time at men's quarters. Without the company of extended family at home they would have felt so lonely and insecure.

These generations had no independence, and empowerment of thought, expression, or action. They were helpless to shape their own lives or that of their children. Women were non-assertive, had low self-esteem, and no self-identity. These traits rather made it easier for males to dominate and financially exploit them. Males were envious of women to grow. So they put constraints for their social mixing with males, recreation, and education. Women felt as being treated more as sex objects by their husbands, and only for producing more and more children. Their life pattern was very stereotyped. This was a life pattern of early marriages, raising large families, and managing home. On the other hand husband would handle and dominate over all other matters, such as children education, marriages, family income/finance and investments, and even interaction with relatives. A woman was treated more of a sex object because of male domination. They had no self-identity at home or outside. They led a totally home-confined life.

They had low opportunities for health care, recreation. No exposure to media or outside world created low awareness and knowledge about the wider world.

There was no sharing of life with husband except sex; that too when he would desire. The major role of women was to produce children. Though she had no say in shaping their (children) lives. Husband was the main decision-maker. She had free say in running the kitchen only. Thus women suffered low self-esteem and loss of identity.

Still life was just 'existence' for them as there was not enough of mental and physical stimulation for upkeep.

Gender Discrimination: There was gender discrimination about food, health care, outdoor recreation, socialization, and education. This bias created a total stunted growth for women. They existed as a different human species.

Education: Women were not sent for formal schooling because of Purdah. In fact, those days there were no schools for girls. Those who were keen for studying; were allowed to study at home. Elderly male teachers would teach them. They would study while sitting behind the Purdah. Direct male interaction was tabooed. Mostly they learnt languages or simple arithmetic. Mainly the women's informal education focus was on household management practicalities, cooking, sewing, and arts and crafts.

Health Care: These women raised large families. Sometimes they would bear eleven to twelve children. Surely they did not want to raise so many children but there were no medical options available to them to limit the births. Their health suffered in the process. 1st and 2nd generation women suffered in health care due to non-availability of women doctors also. They were not allowed contact with male doctors as they were in Purdah. These women mainly used indigenous medicines, and nature cure for common ailments. Women's health suffered because of early marriages, long reproductive years, giving births to number of children, and over and above without proper prenatal, child delivery, or post-natal health care facilities. They had low energy, and suffered early old age symptoms because of long reproductive years and low nutritious diets. Some of them died young if they contacted diseases; but others enjoyed longevity. The secret of their living up to 90's or so might have been due to their self-disciplined life, no tensions of modern life, and enough of physical exercise through house work. Still life was mere existence with nothing to stimulate them.

Marriage: Marriages were arranged according to the family status. The bride and the bridegroom would neither have met or even seen each other. They might be mismatched for age, physical, and mental development, and education. Family had the final say. There were either child or teen marriages. Somehow, these marriages worked. May be because there were no expectations. There were no divorces. If a man did not like his wife, she was just discarded as another sex object. He was free to marry any times he wanted. The discarded wife and her children always lived with the family. The discarded wife was not allowed to remarry.

Widow Status: The incidence of young widows was higher because of early marriages, age incompatibility, and high rate of mortality. Widows were socially and physically tortured. They were treated as ill omen. It was social hypocrisy that widows could not remarry but widowers would marry young unmarried girls. It was social stigma for women to remain unmarried. She had to marry someone even if the groom was disabled, sick, or old person.

Religion: Sanctity was attached to religion. They would try to emulate those religious teachings that they read in holy books in their life. There was more emphasis on rituals and myths rather than religious education *per se*. Some of the religious practices were observed by them to get over the social inhibitions imposed upon them by males. It served as occupation and pastime within the house. In fact the rigid traditions of religion *per se* were really thrust upon them at an early age of 14-15 years when they were not ready for it. Religion was used to discipline young widows' minds from sexual wanderings. Religion was a social ascription to lead their lives in a particular way for widows; for others it was a useful pastime.

Leisure Activities: Arts and crafts flourished through women in homes as generation hand-over. Since they had more time on hand. Reading religious books, and saying prayers were other past time.

Communication Channels: They had interpersonal communication with the immediate members of the family. Communication with husband used to be restrained by conventional tradition of their living in separate quarters. Moreover, women were never consulted for any decision-making. Interpersonal communication with the extended families was occasional. Friendship ties or social networking did not develop since there was no social interaction among women themselves. No mass media channel was available to them. A few of them could read. But the reading was restricted to holy books and scriptures only. Telephones were not available. They could write letters to express themselves; but they were not allowed to do so. Thus they had no media identification.

Perception of 3rd Generation

Lifestyle & Roles: The 3rd generation of women played passive roles in family and society but they were contented with their lives. Most of the women experienced constraining lifestyle in their early childhood and pre-marriage followed by more open lifestyle after marriage. Thus early marriages become solutions to get out of stifling and protected life at parental homes. Before marriage they did not enjoy the freedom of thought and expression, going out unescorted, schooling, and jobs etc. After marriage she led a different style of life as encouraged by the husband. She did not have to observe Purdah. She could interact freely with related males in the family. Since third generation had the advantage of dual life changeovers. In later life when social change allowed them to discard Purdah; they were free to move socially when accompanied by their husbands. There were more interactions with outsiders and males. In urban milieu husbands encouraged wives to share outside lives with them. Many times husband would talk to her about different family matters such as raising children, educating them, and their marriages. They would also share outside life with the husband to some extent. 1st and 2nd generations never got such a chance. They had little exposure to media world. But they were contented with home and family life. The third generation women were respected in their own status as homemakers. They were contented with life but restless in spirit. Such restlessness stimulated higher aspirations for their daughters—the fourth generation.

They were experiencing an underlying and undefined restlessness about not able to do activities which their male counterparts were doing; particularly gaining economic independence, being able to shape their own lives, self-identification, and empowerment. This restlessness created better opportunities for their daughters of the next generations. During this period, some of the women activists achieved these for themselves and struggled hard to achieve the same for their fellow women. Interestingly, male activists joined their struggle for achievement.

The 3rd generation from their experiences realized that to have your own housing shelter gives a great freedom to women. Society will not rent a house to a single woman even if she can afford it. Male relatives will give her shelter, but they would dominate or exploit her. So they encouraged the next generation women to be on their own in order to have the freedom of growth.

Gender Discrimination: The 3rd generation women did have say in the development of their daughters. They did not discriminate between sons and daughters for education, careers, and marriage choices. They guided their daughters to be cautious about career selections to avoid sex exploitation.

Education: In early part of their lives, this generation had no opportunity for education, careers, and employment; and even no choice for marriage. But in second phase of their life many of them did go for higher education when encouraged by husbands. But a negligible number pursued jobs.

Health Care: Throughout the three generations women were bearing large families. Organized health care outside homes has just started to be available to women. Though such curative facilities were available in specific areas only. This was happening because a few women doctors and paramedic were available in urban areas only. Rural women were still suffering. Women had become health conscious.

Marriage: Traditions, caste, community, religion and regions restricted marriage choices. There was no practice of divorce. Wives were just discarded when not liked. Men could marry more than once even when wife was alive. But women had to be tied to one marriage only—good or bad.

Widow Status: There were no legal and social sanctions for widow remarriage among 1st and 2nd generations. But third generation had legal protection and also social support to a little extent. But large families itself was hindrance in remarriage. Widowers had social sanction to marry even with large families.

Religion: Usually among third generation, the religion was saying prayers, temple visits, practicing rituals. They felt such attitude give consistency and integration to family life.

Leisure Activities: They enjoyed more the simple warmth and joys of family life. Women have ushered into this new lifestyle.

Communication Channels: Family members, relatives, and friends relied more on interpersonal communication among themselves. Now they could communicate through post as postal services were available. Print and radio (in 50's) had come on the media scene. They got exposure to national and international news.

Perception of 5th Generation

Lifestyle & Roles: The younger women today are making lot of self-efforts to develop themselves. They are achieving in many directions. They are independent, confident, empowered, and competitive. They are self-centred and know their own mind, egoist, and opinionated. They are not self-effacing. They are concerned about self-identity, and time for self. The perception is that they lack the dignity of life that 4th generation women enjoyed in spite of their struggles for freedom of life. They have freedom of growth, opportunities for education, career, and marriage choices. They have more independence of choice, work, and careers. They are very involved in their careers. They are experiencing better work place environment. Moreover, both men and women are developing healthy attitude towards working women.

Global media exposure has created awareness, information, and knowledge about health, science and technology, arts, politics, and life in general. This influences their lifestyles and growth in general. They have to face so much of competition in every walk of life; that all the time they are running a rat race. They have little time to enjoy what they create and achieve. But they are restless if the life is not challenging.

They cannot live in extended families as they are self-centred, and are not willing to devote much time and effort to nurture those relationships. Whatever extra time they have, they want to spend on self-recreation, socialization, and developing themselves. Whereas their mothers (4th generation) spent more time nurturing extended family relationships. But these extended families are the necessary foundation of family life. Women are not nosey about other women's activities. They have build trust unto themselves. This trust also gives them confidence. Women do not have hypocrite attitude towards life. They are open and straightforward. They have a 'do not care' attitude towards social disapproval.

Gender Discrimination: Girls and boys play, study, and grow up together. No longer there are social inhibitions and constrains for their mixing. They rather develop healthy attitude towards opposite gender. Such an attitude facilitates better life adjustments in life. Parents do not discriminate between sons and daughters as they grow, get education, look for jobs. But at one point, the social set up is biased and obstructs when women tend to outshine males. Women though protected by law still relinquish their parental inheritance of property to brothers. But they do not pass on their husband's inheritance to any one. May be they do so because they have to survive. There is no gender discrimination in employing teachers in co-educational schools. The new trend of having co-educational schools as well as mixed faculty leads to healthy growth of genders.

Education: Women have wider opportunities for pursuing education in multiple disciplines. Co-education developed as an outgrowth of segregated education. This is a healthy development. Professional education also facilitated women to look for professions not totally reserved for males or females. Thus they got wider choices for professional growth.

Health Care: Women are aware of, and have healthy attitude about their own health and fitness, and also that of the family. As compared to them, the older generations were health and nutrition conscious but more for the family than for themselves. In fact, they used to totally ignore their own health demands. They did make fewer efforts to beauty-groom themselves, and would use only homemade cosmetics. The young women are conscious about physical beauty and frequent beauty parlors for it. Fitness centers are also frequented because they are getting figure conscious too.

The awareness, availability, and accessibility to medical facilities have created better health status for these women. Moreover, there are no social constraints for consulting male doctors; it is their personal choice. General tensions, sedentary jobs, modern household gadgetry, and low quality of environment are the secondary factors that cause health concerns.

Marriage: Women have opportunities to make independent marriage choices. There are less social restrictions. They go steady before marriage. Dating is still not personally and socially approved. They have fewer inhibitions about sex, and do not have hypocrite attitude about it. On the whole marriages are stable and sharing. When it does not work, mutual divorce is the solution for it. Divorcee marriages are socially approved.

Widow Status: Widows have social status and command respect. Socially, they are not ill treated. A widow need not live with her parents. She can set up her own home. They can remarry if they choose. Society and laws approve it. Laws protect her inheritance of husband's property and money. Even if she is not earning herself, she has something to fall back and does not have to depend on others' mercy. This gives her confidence and social status.

Religion: Religion is a matter of choice, convenience, and moral conviction. Emphasis is on good values of life. It is a philosophy of life that is unique for every one since it assimilates in the lifestyle. Rituals are not compulsory and they are more for social interactions. The serious religious bend usually starts when they are in 30's.

Leisure Activities: These are varied from sports to arts and crafts, and to all kind of live and media entertainment. Sharing time with family is also important activity. The wholesome feeling is that in life, leisure activities are equally important as primary work.

Communication Channels: Electronic media channels are predominant in their lifestyles. These have globalisation impact. Interpersonal communication channels links are also favoured.

Generation Transition Period

The process of social change across women generations brought a transition period in sixties. The social and legal concerns of modernization led to change for betterment of women's life in many spheres. The generations were transforming through the process of social change. The male counterparts developed healthy attitude and behaviour particularly to tolerate and respect newly accorded freedom to women.

Women status improved when she became independent economically, socially, and emotionally. She resented male domination. The women have searched for their identity across generations and have achieved it. The advancements in technology have improved their lifestyles and health. Women developed across generations through each generation's struggles and sacrifices; especially those of 3rd generation. The aggressiveness of the 4th generation stimulated the 5th generation to achieve. Now society is tolerant of women independence, and it is somewhat safe for her to move unescorted without being sexually harassed. No longer there is social stigma to widows or divorcees remarriage. They have social dignity. Women have legal sanctions to inherit parental property but due to low social support they relinquish their rights in favour of male members of the family for fear of family disintegration. Modernity, education, outside employment, wider media networks and media influences have changed the generations' lifestyles through passage of time. The changes in social values occurred by exposure to modernity, wider media networks, and legislation to protect women rights.

Development Point

The restlessness of women themselves, the understanding of the younger male generations, and national and international media exposures stimulated and created channels of growth for women.

Women's own efforts and assertiveness, economic independence, and being in workforce were steps towards developing themselves. The government efforts focusing on both social and technological developments to give quality of life to women, and reckon them as a social and manpower force further gave impetus to their development. The political will, social legislation, women's struggle, sacrifices, and efforts to achieve social justice have all contributed to their developments. Religion has changed overtime from superstitions, myths, rituals, and conventional morality to an honest way of life.

The 5th generation does not suffer eve teasing, as society has become more tolerant of women's independence. But other different kind of crimes against them has come up. This generation has gained from the sacrifices and experiences of older 4th generation. Parents have encouraged them to grow through exposure to wide variety of opportunities. They have become mature and wiser due to parental guidance, conventional wisdom, media exposure, and wider opportunities created by post-modernity. Laws provide that women can inherit property and money these days. Parents still prefer sons to inherit. The inheritance laws give her the right but invariably she relinquishes her right on social demand. In fact, equal amount of money and efforts are being spent in upbringing daughters and sons. The healthy trend is that widow and divorcee remarriages are legally and socially acceptable.

Women of 3rd generation had less confined life as compared to 2nd generation because of British influence in India that was pro-women, and due to the impact of urbanization and modernization. They stimulated better lives for their daughters of 4th generation by their own restlessness of spirit, and aspirations. The 5th generation women benefited the most from advancement of technology in different fields. As compared to other generations, 2nd generation had the hardest time devoid of all household electric or electronic technology.

The 3rd generation made sacrifices, and they struggled hard to achieve their righteous place in society through legislation. Whereas the 4th generation made tremendous efforts to get social support for these laws protecting women's rights. Legislation, political will, efforts of male and female activists, global media exposure, and efforts and will of women themselves helped in creating an identity for them.

5

WOMEN IN DIALOGUE: FIFTH GENERATION WOMEN

Group 3: Twenty-five Plus Age Group

Generation Perspective: Self-Perception

Lifestyle & Roles: The open, and healthy environment, freedom of movement, and experiences of parents have all contributed to balance growth. A healthy environment is created when both the parents are educated and working. Such growth has resulted in development of assertiveness and achievement orientation among women of this generation. Parents did encourage active academic and cultural participation. We have less social inhibitions as our parents and social set up encouraged gender intermixing from childhood to work. We welcome parental guidance in education, career, and marriage choices even. What we do strongly resent is their domination and making decisions for us; as we like to grow independent. Even after marriage, we like to share life with husband and not be dominated by him.

We are better-informed citizens because of our own efforts and external forces; because of wider technological opportunities, and global connectivity. There is more information, awareness, and knowledge.

Our lifestyles have changed in modes of dress, the types of food, housing, recreation, entertainment, and social interaction etc. These have changed to become more functional. Exposure to global media has brought western cultural convergence. These changes have affected our thinking, attitudes, and beliefs. This process of social change has influenced the development of women *per se.*

Women can grow well if not dominated by parents or in-laws. They must set up their own goals in life, and priorities, to achieve them. Parental guidance is all right but when parents in their enthusiasm dominate every decision; it kills the initiative.

Women are developing the capabilities to make their own decisions, and decisions for their families. In family roles, they share decision-making with husbands for themselves, children life, education, household management etc. These are mutual decisions but taken according to each other's capabilities. Women are playing significant and active role in politics, and community affairs.

Gender Discrimination: We were (are being) given the same type of upbringing, education, career choices, and marriage choices as given to our brothers. The government also made the same kind of efforts to provide facilities for lifestyle, education, professions, and work etc. for both male and females. There were no discriminations. Society endorsed it also. Sexes were not segregated (as in 4th generation). Gender intermixing was encouraged both by the parents and society; though there were prescribed boundaries. Parents or society does not tolerate sexual permissiveness in order to give dignity to women.

We do not experience bias against us in work place or professional choices, or wages etc. or in social attitude and behaviour. There is less sexual harassment at work places or in public. But there is an inkling that women have to work twice hard to go up very high up the career ladder in spite of the fact they may have the merits. This happens may be because men are jealous of women independence and professional growth. In fact, the young men feel threatened when women strive for parity. In senior professional positions; women get less recognition for their merits.

On the other hand, women are getting more social and legislation protection to achieve parity with men. Women are winning their point when they are assertive, aggressive, and are bonding together against gender discrimination.

Education: We have got wider choices in variety of educational disciplines. Many professional courses are open to us. We have co-education from school to universities. Professionally also there is no gender segregation in professions or work place. There is low discrimination in wages. The male chauvinistic attitude cannot tolerate women outshining them in profession. It is a blow to women's self-esteem. This generation even aspires for higher and professional education for their own children, which must fit to their aptitudes and capabilities. We feel that we were pushed to many professional choices by our parental choices and aspirations. Most women work primarily for professional interest, economic independence, to improve quality of life, and gain self-confidence. Most try to balance family and work, which is imperative for smooth running of families. It may be stressful at times but they accept this challenge.

New legislation has created wider educational opportunities such as compulsory and free school education, opening of more colleges, and providing facilities to women for professional skill development. The legislation has also protected women in work places with regard to wages, and affording fair opportunities for them professionally. Women have been trying their best to avail the opportunities and facilities thus created.

Health Care: This generation is enjoying better health care facilities. Advance medical technologies, qualified female and male doctors and other paramedics, and good hospital infrastructures have created facilities for cure for many illnesses. The awareness, knowledge, and their own efforts give them access to preventive measures to ward off many illnesses. Further, the availability and accessibility of family planning devices help them in planning and spacing their families. This improves quality of life both for the families as well for the nation. There is overall improvement in consciousness about health, and nutrition.

Marriage: Mostly marriages are facilitated. Women have 'a say' in mate selection. There are no caste and community restrictions. Even there is less rigidity for inter-regional marriages. International and intercultural marriages are almost negligible but are tolerated. Women go steady after engagement. Dating system is not encouraged and practiced.

Children are necessary for cementing marriage relationships. We are aware of the overpopulation in the country and its consequences. There is no particular preference for sons. But one or two children are necessary. We believe in quality upbringing of children.

Sanctity is attached to marriage. But they break on many counts which early generations did not face and experienced. Marriages mainly break on incompatibility and intoleration. Incompatibility has different connotation now than in earlier generations. It may be about her professional identity or her self-esteem. Mental cruelty or physical violence can be other factors. But this generation is the only one that faces divorce due to social violence such as dowry demands, or childless marriages etc. When they break, they do not want any intervention from parents (though parents are willing to intervene on this count). They feel confident to deal with it themselves. They may seek counselling from close friends. Marriage counsellors are rare. Family is the main catharsis. Thus divorce gets both legal and strong social support. Still they do not break on flimsy grounds. Since they have legal sanction to divorce by mutual agreement; they do not drag it long in courts, or indulge in public mud slinging; since they do want to restart their life. Divorce seems to be a healthier way to get out of incompatible marriages.

Many women do suffer in marriage relationships because of mother-in-law's intolerance. They suffer through 'woman-to-woman cruelty' syndrome. Government also set up woman cells and legal aid cells to help women (without resources) against cruelty, and enforcement of their rights. The general feeling is that the staff in the woman cells is not empathetic and trained to deal with women's issues rather they harass the complainants. More and more educated women from good families should volunteer to help in these cells.

Women are assertive and aggressive about anti-dowry demands. They feel humiliated by such demands. It is evil when parents are coerced and forced to pay dowry. Many women suffered and were burnt alive because of dowry; it was legally banned. But social awareness is imperative. Marriage laws protect them against many ills related to marriage, such as child marriages, polygamy, Sati, dowry. They encourage remarriage, inheritance of property and money, divorce etc.

Widow remarriage is encouraged both by law and socially. They command respect and life as a human being. Men have double standard towards divorcee remarriages. Divorced men would remarry an unmarried or widow but they would hesitate to remarry a divorcee. On the whole, there is social support for divorcee remarriages.

Religion: Our generation believe in honest and simple living. There is no hypocrisy. The focus is on observing good values of life. Religious environment given by families in early childhood creates good grounding for honest values and stable personality. Religious discipline is good but not something to be imposed at any age. It has to come from within. Our generation does observe some festivals and rituals and occasional visits to the temple.

Leisure Activities: More leisure time is spent with immediate family, with children in active sports, media entertainment, recreation, and cultural activities. Women balance work, family, and leisure within the time limitations. That is why they look forward to spending quality time in leisure.

Attitude to Technology: Technology has given global inter-connectivity for over all lifestyles and roles such as in education, work, play, entertainment, and at home. Technology has provided to women more information, awareness, and knowledge about varied fields. This has stimulated them for achieving higher.

Politics: Many women of our generation are participating in active politics. It is a must. Active politics will give voice to them; otherwise they are ignored, or heard through the male voices, or their concerns are given low priority. Women are involving more and more in community affairs. Such active involvement gives them hold on improving the day to day living environment; and making demands to improve the quality of life for women as such.

Communication Channels: The rapid technological changes overtime have more media channels for communication. These have created better inter-connectivity at local, national and international levels in all spheres of life. Interpersonal communications have improved from only personal to varied impersonal networks.

Inter-Generation Perspective: Other Perception

Lifestyle & Roles: The lifestyles of our mothers' generation (4th generation) contributed towards creating balanced growth for us. It gave us freedom of movement with boundaries and trust. We benefited a balanced attitude towards life. This generation of women had mixed growth opportunities. Some grew up with confidence, assertiveness, and with good hold on their family life. This happened because males in their life gave them freedom and stimulation to grow whereas others were dominated by their husbands. They provided them with all comforts of life, and respected them but they would not allow them to have any say in any matter. Thus these women had low self-esteem, and they were not assertive. Since they were educated, they could always fall back on it in times of need; and it did give them confidence to handle complexities of life.

Our grandmothers (3rd generation) had cloistered parental protected life till they were married in their teens. Later, their husbands encouraged them to come out of their shells and share life with them. Thus they strived for different lifestyle and gender roles; especially whatever has been denied to them in their earlier phase of life. They gained control over their own lives, and over their family. Later, such a control goaded their daughters to achieve more. In fact they were experiencing the process of social change.

Our great grandmothers (1st & 2nd generations) felt helpless because of male domination. They had no empowerment because they were not educated, they had no economic independence, and no interaction with the outside world. Male perception of woman was only to provide her for her physical needs. He would make efforts to provide her food, clothes, shelter, and sex (according to his needs); but her psycho and emotional needs were totally ignored otherwise.

Gender Discrimination: The earlier three generations' women suffered acute gender bias in all aspects of their life such as freedom to growth, and to express their thoughts. She had no separate identity of her own from males in her family. They guided and dictated her life—the father, brother, and husband.

The process of social change brought more openness and freedom to the life of fourth generation.

They did not suffer gender bias in education, work, life-styles and roles, and entertainment to a greater extent. But they did face certain limitations. The third generation in their second phase of life started experiencing the openness of societal changes and was fired with a restless spirit to get those opportunities to their daughters.

Marriage: Our mothers had no say in 'who' they would marry. Marriages were mainly arranged according to region, community, and status of the family. Since women were getting educated; the educational parity was additional criterion. A few marriages were facilitated also. Parents' choice was final. As a change, woman was allowed to meet the fiancee a few times before marriage with escort.

Public policies and legislation were protecting women against child marriages, polygamy, and bigamy. There was legal sanction for divorce. But many would not opt for it, as there was no social support. Divorcees or divorced remarriages were not given social acceptance. But widow remarriage was gaining social status. Their anti-dowry attitude was passive only as they could not play aggressive role in defending themselves. At times they had to suffer indignities on this account also.

Our grandmothers (3rd generation) were not protected by law against child marriages, polygamy etc. Marriages were arranged according to caste, community, region, and social status of the family. Age and occupation of the groom was considered. Education parity of the groom and bridegroom was not a criterion. Married life was different for this generation in second phase of their life.

They could not divorce if they were not happy in marriage relationships. They suffered the whims of men, through mental and physical cruelty. They had no respite from it as they could neither divorce nor remarry. Widows too had to lead a dependent life. They were not allowed to remarry. They had to put up with physical, mental, and social cruelty.

These women did not have to face the menace of dowry. Since this was treated more as gift giving only. The social attitude was very different. Women were never maltreated on account of dowry. In those days even the number of wedding gifts was socially fixed.

The first and second generations also suffered the same destiny but with more sufferings as they were forced to lead a very cloistered life.

Health Care: Our mothers enjoyed better health facilities both preventive and curative then our grandmothers and great grandmothers. The reasons were, they did not have to suffer the social taboos of Purdah, and only being allowed to consult female doctors. Moreover, the second phase of their life was more open. They had more awareness and knowledge about health due to both media and interpersonal communication channels reach. These channels were neither available nor accessible to earlier generations.

Religion: Religion was a way of life, and essential past time for our great grandmothers since they were confined to four walls of the house, with little else to do. It was even hypocrisy when imposed on their lifestyles. They were superstitious, and fatalistic in attitude. They observed the festivals and ritual for social gatherings and expressing social inhibitions.

Our grandmothers (3rd generation) were having comparatively more open attitude to religion. They were less ritualistic, though they did observe festivals enthusiastically.

Our mothers identified religion with good values of life. They observed only the essential rituals and festivals.

Leisure Activities: Our great grandmothers and grandmothers developed arts and crafts, and even culinary art in their leisure time. These activities they could pursue in the privacy of their homes and were self learnt. In fact they were taught and handed over to the generations. They were great artists. It gave them happiness in creating these arts.

Our mothers have less time to pursue these. Their leisure time pursuits were educational, family related roles, sports, media recreation, professional, and outside social activities.

Society at this point has to offer more and she has to grab more.

Attitude to Technology: The earlier generations always had open attitude to technology in any sphere of their life. Much depended on the availability, and reach of these technologies to them. Over a period of time, these technologies have made their life easier and more connected.

Communication Channels: The reach of media channels and even more sophisticated interpersonal communication channels have a long journey from 1st to present 5th generation. The technology has facilitated it and made its scope wider. The earlier generations did not enjoy the connectivity of public communication *per se* nor lifestyles of some of the generations permitted.

Generation Transition

The process of social change that started in the decades of 60's and 70's and in the beginning of life of 3rd and 4th generations has brought positive benefits for present younger generations. The awareness thus created has transited younger women of today into independent human beings. They are enjoying a greater degree of self-identity and self-esteem. They have gained in personality, values, and achievements. They are assertive, aggressive, and bonding together to win rights for themselves and against any gender discriminations. The process of social change supported by legal provisions has accelerated the transition.

The education and parental open attitude paved better life for daughters. Parents have experienced gender discriminations to some extent; therefore they were not willing to tolerate and allow gender biases for their daughters. Open social environment, wider opportunities for growth—such as education, careers, marriage choices and protections etc. over the generations have made these women more conscious of their rights, as well assertive and aggressive to achieve them. Basically they are achievers and they had been able to preserve the dignity and identity which the third and fourth generations struggled hard to gain.

Development Point

The contributing factors to development of the fifth generation of women were many and based on the struggles of their mothers and grandmothers, wider opportunities, legal redresses and sanctions, public policies, social support, and overall efforts of the women themselves.

Wider opportunities, legal, and social support for girls' education and more so for professional education opened wider professional choices. Women aspired for it and felt the need to develop them. More educational and career openings are giving self-confidence to women to grow. The economic independence thus gained developed self-identity for women. The geographic and professional mobility created impetus for further growth. The women made efforts themselves, they adopted an aggressive attitude not to be discriminated and exploited by males and society.

More and more legal redresses of women's problems, and higher social support to legal sanctions have let them develop. Legal and social support to divorce has given a new acquired dignity to them. The inheritance laws have given them control over their own life and that of their family.

The present trends in development of women are posing numerous challenges to them also.

6

PROFILES: INDIAN WOMEN

People think narratively rather than argumentatively and pragmatically. Research shows that knowledge is communicated most effectively through a convincing narrative that is delivered with formal elegance and passion. There is meaningful link between stories and knowledge—the way they embody experience, apply to future expectations. They are based in feelings and thoughts. It is something that resonates with other people. These can be constructed retrospectively, but can be used prospectively.

We Map the Profiles of Five Generations Through Narratives

Our research analysis of these narratives reveals that the five generations differed in their lifestyles, and roles they played in the family and in the outer world. They differed over time in opportunities, societal attitudes to education, careers, health care, marriage and related issues like selection of mate, divorce, widow status and remarriages and polygamy; towards leisure activities and entertainment; and religion and religious practices. Gender discrimination was the key point that affected the life of women in all the above spheres.

Our research is a pointer to the fact that Indian women have developed positively during this century. The process of social change, global media technology and advancement, the National Political Will, the national legislation, the international efforts, and women's own efforts have all played key roles.

Our conclusions present holistic scenario for women through past generations, identifying number of open issues, new research agenda, and communication strategies. We face the challenge of finding appropriate balance between our experiences of our own selves as women; and our common experiences as human beings. Further, renegotiating this balance through the pursuits of various development goals.

We have described the biography of generations. It looks at history through the windows of a single generation as it ages. What it reveals is dealing with the growth strains of generations. It is the biography of generations raised among the confines of four walls, and their great expectations from life. The past generations of Indian women since 1900 may be history but they have incredible implications for us all—the future generations.

We present the changeovers through women generations by a composite scenario.

Changing Generations: A Composite Scenario

The composite scenario highlights the salient changeovers on an ascending scale of growth through generations:

* Lifestyles changed from living a cloistered life to an open life. The helplessness of women changed to empowerment. Women had no identity, but they achieved self-identity. There was total segregation of genders; gender mixing in various spheres is a normal way of life now. Women had no say and control over family; she controls and balances family and work. Technology-oriented life both at home and work gives her more time and leisure for herself and family.
* Women's roles in life changed. They were not assigned any public roles; now they enjoy multiple roles in public life. They had no role in the family to play but now they control the family significantly. They had no say in the social set up—they have upgraded from no social role to social activators demanding change. They were helpless socially; now they accept challenges of their development in politics, community, and family. They have upgraded from helplessness to control, sharing, decision-making, and management in all spheres of life. They were not able to take any professions; now they are competing in higher professional roles both with males and females.

* Women's achievements spiralled. They were illiterate; now they are highly educated in general as well in many professions. The professional growth has led to wider professional choices; whereas earlier she was a mere homemaker and no entity. She had no say who her marriage partner would be; now she had the freedom to choose her marriage partner without caste, community, and regional restrictions. She died without seeing a doctor; now she gets good health care to enjoy good health and longevity. Being confined to the house, household chores, and religious rituals were her only leisure activity; but now she enjoys a wide variety of outdoor and indoor leisure activities without any gender discriminations. She has achieved self-esteem, social status, and economic independence through support of law and society. It is a big changeover; she was devoid of all these. Her biggest achievement is that she had the protection of legislation and reformers to develop from non-entity to an achiever in all basic spheres of life such as education, profession, marriage, health care, economic independence, and above all in gaining self-esteem.
* Crimes against women have increased. Sex exploitation, domestic and social violence, rape, molestation, and call girls prostitution has increased as the women have come out of the shell of protected home lives. They have to suffer the indignities of crimes against them in the external world as they move and live alone unprotected. The law may protect them more and more. But what is needed is the male toleration and respect for women's freedom.
* Communication perspectives have changed through generations. What woman communicates, through what channels, who is her audience, and the effect of her communication have undergone significant changes overtime.

Women communicated about themselves, their family and extra familial concerns. Later, as their horizons widened, they communicated about political, community, work place, and international concerns about women in general. The patterns and the channels of communication for interaction, information, and knowledge have differed from generation to generation. The emphasis has shifted from informal interpersonal to local and national mass media channels; and further to formal interpersonal and global mass media channels. The use and style of interpersonal channels can be attributed to social structural changes in women lifestyles across generations (from 1st & 2nd generations of early 20th century through the 5th generation of today). It transformed when the transition was from home confined life to wider external social networking among men and women. The media exposure transition was partly due to advancement of technology and partly its wider access to women in general. Figure 6.1 shows the tiers of patterns of communication.

It will be interesting to know the patterns of how women expressed grievances about themselves and life in general, to whom, and with what effect. These patterns did change across generations. The 1st and 2nd generations were passive complainers because of their unique social constraints, low access to interpersonal channels and non-availability of media channels to them. The 3rd generation was mixed in their approach—sometimes passive, sometimes loud; they were pushing and restless to stimulate next generation both through interpersonal and mass media channels which were accessible and available to some extent. The 4th and the 5th generations are active complainers, self-dependent, and looking for strategies, solutions and implementation. They have the advantage of global media channels and wider interpersonal channels. These created challenges for them to transform their lives in the changing world. This is true of the 5th generation to a greater extent.

On the whole, currently the different communication perspectives effect women lifestyles. They have a say in the home matters; at home the interpersonal communication is interactive and multiways. At office they are in control; interpersonal and technological channels help them in communicating within and outside the organization. In societal matters now they communicate their concerns, they make decisions, and demand structural changes. They use both interpersonal and media channels to be effective at societal

Generation	Expression channels	Outcome	Redress by
1st and 2nd Generations →	• Women to women in the extended family • None ↔	• Frustration • Fatalism • Depression • Suicides • Detachment • Loneliness ↔	• Depends on attitude of Male & Female, Family members
3rd Generation →	• Women in extended family • Husband, sons male member in the family ↔	• Better grip on life • Sharedness to some extent • Participation in family life ↔	• Husband have more open attitude • Sons • Grandsons
4th Generation →	• Husband, parents, children • Male and Female relatives • Male and Female colleagues • Forums Women and general media ↔	• Vocal visibility • Sharedness • Participation in family in-groups and outside groups to express grievances ↔	• Self, parents, husband • Male and female relative; colleague • Socio political organisations forums of women general Media
5th Generation →	• Parents, husband, children • Male and Female relatives • Male and Female colleagues • Forums, organizations, women in general ↔	• Vocal visibility • Sharedness • Participation in family, in-groups, outside groups • Active involvement in finding solutions ↔	• Self, parents, husband • Male and female relative; colleague • Socio political organisations, forums of women media

Fig. 6.1: Tiers of Communication Across Generations.

Fig. 6.1 shows how women expressed grievances about their own life, to whom, and with what effect. The Ist and 2nd generations were passive complainers because of their unique constraints. 3rd generation was mixed. The 4th and 5th generations were active complainers, self-dependent and looking for strategies, solutions and implementations.

level. Their communication efforts to project their concerns, demands, strategies and solutions both through interpersonal and media channels to the government are effective in focusing on women development issues. The total effect of various communication perspectives in women lifestyles has attracted global media attention, created awareness about changing women perspectives around the world, and the urgent need to deal with women concerns and development issues.

THE SALIENT MESSAGE IS: WOMEN CANNOT BE IGNORED ANY MORE

Recommendations and Future Directions for Research

In the study of Women Across Generations our arguments and counter arguments rest on commonality among generations; but there are distinctions within the population worth-noting. Women within a generation have grown in different ways such as their vital sensibility because of socio-economic and rural-urban differences. The process of social change has affected women across generations. Cultural specific milieu and boundaries affect generations across cultures. A few salient studies are recommended for future research:

1. It is recommended to study specific group of women generations for wider implications and generalizations.
2. To draw profiles of women across generations through analysis of media—print, films, television and folklore.
3. A content analysis of distinguished women's lifestyles to tell us about the turning points in their life.
4. Research on focal points of reforms taken up by women and men social activists for women development during a specific period.
5. Research in policies for women development and their impact.
6. Policy dialogue between gender researchers, policy-makers, and activists to make socio-economic policies, and productive processes more accountable to women.
7. Research on some of the key areas identified as obstacles to the advancement of women such as access to, and participation in definition of economic, structural policies, and productive processes; and the

institutional mechanisms to promote the advancement of women.

This book is not about the 'generation gap' but a journey through generations. We conclude our journey with an optimistic note.

7

SALIENT NARRATIVES

THIRD GENERATION

Group 1: Narrative 1

I am 86 years old. But I am depressed and disillusioned with life and I am waiting for life to pass away. I feel lonely and isolated as everybody in the family is so busy and involved in their own family units. They may want to do things for me, help me in different ways but I like to be independent. I enjoy being like that, and enjoy my ways and I do not like to be dependent on others.

I feel lonesome and worthless not because people are not around me but because due to physical disability I cannot go out and interact with outsiders to handle my finances and other mundane matters. In addition, when you go out you are aware of the changing scenarios in the society. I am quite intelligent, sharp, articulate, and have good management sense. But I am afraid to move out of the house lest somebody pushes me down the road; as somebody did once. These days the younger generation is in so much hurry that they do not care for older people.

For years I have been enjoying the freedom of movement, decision-making and being a powerful figure in my household. This could happen because my husband encouraged me to be independent and in fact taught me how to handle financial and outside matters. This has paid dividends. I have been widow for the last 26 years but I do not have to depend on anybody. My husband had great respect for women independence.

I have not been to school. In those days girls from rich families were not sent to school but I was taught at home to read and write Hindi and simple mathematical calculations. I enjoy reading and writing even now. In those days young girls were not allowed to go out of the house for fear of sexual exploitation. Whenever they had to go out it always had to be under heavy veil, and they could travel only in heavily curtained and fully escorted carriages. I wish those days women had access to education at school. I would have been brilliant in studies since I have such sharp brain. The extended family life and its intrigues did teach me about the practicalities of life, and how to handle them.

At fourteen I was married. I have no sweet memories of my childhood. We were cooped up in the house like prisoners. No outings, no books, no magazines to read, no television or radio to watch, no friends to interact with, and no innocent joys of life to cherish. As girls, we were not even allowed to talk loudly. Whereas, I could see from the windows of house, the boys including my brother shouting, playing, and running carefree. But I did become adept in embroidery that was an art that women generations handed over to their daughters and grand-daughters. Now-a-days this art is dying because the younger women of today do not want to learn it; a few who have learnt it are commercializing it which is good. I always heard in my childhood, my mother and grandmother saying that being woman was a curse. They felt helpless and unhappy; still they could not do anything to break those shackles and make their daughters happy and less helpless.

It seems that my growing over to adolescent was just a waiting period for marriage. I was learning the practicality of household management and married life. That way the young women of those days were much mature in these respects than women of today. I was lucky to be married to a person with good education and matching my age. Otherwise in those days even parents used to marry their girls of 14 years to 40 years old men with children. The widower could thus remarry even a child bride. But even the young widows without children were not allowed to remarry. Though I do not know what use to be the criteria for such match making—the wealth or the respectability of the families. But for men, the criteria were always physical beauty and the youth of the bride. Those helpless child brides were thus shifted from bad to worse environments. Interestingly, in those days men were well educated but they did not mind getting married to low educated or even illiterate women.

The good point was that my life completely changed after marriage. Though it did not happen for all. To tell you frankly I enjoyed my womanhood only after marriage since I got opportunities to bloom for three good reasons. One, now I was living in urban, modern, British influenced environment of Delhi, as my husband was a journalist there. Life was more open for women in Delhi. Second, I did not have to live in extended family of my in-laws otherwise I had to observe all the social taboos; and life would have been stifling again. Third, my husband was very understanding and encouraged me to grow in life along with him.

If I look back, I feel good about my life after marriage. I even fulfilled my dreams of highly educating my daughters, making them work for careers of their choice, giving them opportunities to go steady and interact with their would be husbands before marriage, though we parents arranged the match. Thus these were arranged marriages with a difference. The most I enjoyed was that my daughters could take me into confidence when they were growing up. They could share their good and bad days with me. I was and am their friend. This never happened when I was growing up. My mother and grandmother and other family members would treat me as 'alien', and 'not belonging to this family'. Thus love, affection, sharedness, and the sense of belongingness were never inculcated within the family. I too felt at that time that after marriage I truly would belong to my in-laws' family. Those days the young girls would dream for love, affection, sharedness, and belongingness from their future family only. But ironically they could seldom get that. Mostly they would be mistreated or stifled by women in-laws. Thus young women would never bloom. I observe that these days mothers-in-law are more tolerant of their daughters-in-law. Moreover, the daughters-in-law are also quite aggressive and assertive and do not tolerate any interference in their lives.

These days the health and medical care is much better and accessible to women. There are women doctors available. Women themselves are conscious of their health and eat nutritious food. After marriage though I was living in urban areas, the medical facilities in general were not that good and far less for women as such. There were hardly any hospitals. The midwives delivered babies at home. Mainly indigenous Indian medicine system like Ayurved and home made medicinal recipes were practiced for common diseases. But for serious illnesses like Tuberculosis cures were not available as medical technology was not that advanced. Comparatively, women used more home made herbal medicines like neem, turmeric, basil, ginger etc. This was same in my mother's times. In early days women use to bear many children. Too many childbirth, and miscarriages used to affect the health of the women but there were no diagnostic, preventive, or curative measures available. They used to suffer and then die at an early age. But those who survived those travails did live long. These days the young women bear only one or two children for many reasons. The major concern is overpopulation of the country both at individual and government levels. Secondly, it is hard to bring up many children in today's world when cost of living is high and parents' aspire high for their children. Moreover, with both the parents working to make both ends meet where do they have time to look after more than two children. Luckily, these days, the family planning devices are also available to limit the family. Whereas, in my time or in my mother's and grandmother's time, in spite of the fact that women did not wish that many children, they had to bear them, abort them, or suffer ill health, as well lead a life with less comforts for the family.

I became widow when I was sixty years. Widowhood was not a curse to me like that for my grandmother, mother or for women of those days. In those days, they were deprived of even the essentials of life. They were not given good, nourishing food to eat. Non-vegetarian food was total taboo. They had to wear white clothes only and were not allowed to wear woolen clothes in winter. They could not wear any jewelry. They had to shave their heads etc. The idea was not so much as that they would be thus observing mourning for their dead husbands but rather that they should not be sexually attractive to other male members of the extended family. Social participation in any of the festivities or rituals was taboo for these widows as they were considered ill omen.

As a widow, I never felt helpless or less empowered to do things for my children, family, friends or myself. I had independence of decision-making and taking action; and did not have to depend totally on male help. I had status in society and society respected me. I participated in social functions and festivities where I was always respected. I had the freedom to dress.

Religion or religious rituals were women's domain. Mainly women and girls used to participate in these practices within the house. Religious rituals, festivities, marriages and other ritualistic social functions would give chance to women to get together, sing, and dance and throw away all inhibitions. Men would participate in these functions only for a short time. Saying daily prayers, worshipping idols in the home was also a good pastime for my mother and grandmother. It also gave them focus to forget their helplessness in life; and rationalizing everything as God's Will. I do have religious bend of mind as influenced by my early childhood environment but I do not spend hours and hours daily saying prayers.

I feel good about my achievements in life. Today in 90's, women of younger generation like my grand-daughter are a mixed lot. First, they are confused about what they want to be in life—career women, homemaker or both. They are lucky to have wide opportunities. But both these roles are demanding. Moreover, I have observed that demanding, competition oriented multiple roles create emotional and physical stress for these women. In the midst of all, they lack the supporting services of extended family (they do not want to live in extended family also) to lend hand in taking care of household, children and socialization. When exasperated, she aptly longs for reversal of roles, and comments that her mother and grandmother's life was better than hers, and they were happier than she is!

Certainly they were happier. Though they were not better placed in life. Life was not competitive and demanding; nor it gave them wide and global opportunities to grow. Happiness, and achieving more are relative terms that change conceptually as women move from one generation to another, from one time to another. Flashbacks of my life tell me that comparatively, my grandmother and mother's generations were not happy in the true sense however contented they might have been. I feel my generation was striving for many things in life that they had been denied so far. Therefore, they were restless to begin with, happier as life passed on, but not contented totally with what they achieved. Their aspirations were higher for generations to come. My daughter's generation is perhaps the best-placed generation so far. My granddaughters are striving ahead of all generations in many respects and achieving more and more due to global exposures. But they are confronted with challenges on many fronts.

There is always a big question mark—are we women, in any generation, leading a productive life? Do we have our separate identities or they are merged with the family or social identities?

Narrative 2

I am in my eighties but I feel wonderful in health and enjoying the best of urban Delhi life specially basking in the sun that is very invigorating. Oh it is so different from my childhood. Talking about my early life as a young girl; most of the time I had to remain inside the house. Those days girls were not sent to schools. But I learnt to read and write at home. My father and brother encouraged me, my mother was indifferent to it. The society did not permit otherwise my father would have sent me to school (there were not even girls schools).

My father was the decision-maker in the house for outside matters and financial matters. My mother and other women living in the house were respected a lot. Kitchen and house were their domain. Those days most of the homes including mine never had television, radio, newspapers, telephones. Women were not allowed to have any friendship networks even among the women. So women kept themselves busy with the household chores, taking care of children, and saying their prayers. In fact religion was the exclusive domain of women. I never saw my father or brother saying prayers or visiting temple. Of course women could not visit temples publicly. It was only on occasions like festivals, weddings, and other social rituals that women could visit the temples exclusively. It was only in these social and religious functions that women could intermix with women friends and relatives, sing and dance, and throw away all the inhibitions. Even the language of our folk songs is suggestive. Apart from family male relatives, women's day-to-day contact with other males included domestic servants, priests, and vendors (who would visit the house to sell clothes, jewelry, and cosmetics).

In those days women were healthier, they ate well and also got good physical exercise from the type of household work they used to do. They would observe cleanliness and hygiene in the kitchen and houses. These days, women are conscious of nutritious food but they are too finicky about it and land up in not eating well. Moreover, as such there is food adulteration now-a-days. The end result is that women are not as healthy in spite of advance medical technology and knowledge. Young girls had to observe Purdah (remain behind the veils). I could not even play outside in the open. Playing with boys was tabooed. Any interactions with men were not allowed. But still I grew up among warm family relationships. I envied my brothers who could go to school to learn, could freely play, and move about outside the house.

I am proud mother of seven children but I am more proud of my two sons that I got after my five daughters were born. I am not anti daughters but it is necessary to have sons since they look after the parents in old age. You need them more for physical, emotional security and not so much for financial security. Ours is an extended family and I enjoy living with my sons' families. I do not feel lonely at all, I love playing with my grandchildren and enjoy the company of my daughters-in-law.

I know these days every one opt for two children family only for various reasons especially because of population explosion in the country. My sons have also two children each. But one must have a son. Personally, I believe in large family if one can afford it. It gives children a sense of family belongingness and integrity.

I will say women of my age enjoy better life these days as they have independence, empowerment, and respect. They have both social and legal rights to lead more open lives and not constrained in the homes by force. The younger generation women too are enjoying this kind of life. In addition, they have access to wide variety of educational fields, career choices, and they are doing well. Even they have marriage choices. Marriages are no longer arranged. Mostly, either they choose their own partners or they have say in doing so. Less and less community, region, and caste restrictions are being observed for mate selection.

Women have developed more through passage of time. They are not only good in offices but they are growing up as good homemakers, and bringing up their children well. But these demanding multiple roles do not leave enough time for themselves, or to nurture husband-wife relationships. That is why divorce and breaking up of the families is on the increase. It happens when they cannot cope up with the tensions. Of course dowry and domestic violence are other reasons for divorce. In our times, there was different type of sanctity attached to marriages. Good or bad women used to stick to marriages. May be they had no option. But now women have economic independence. They quit marriage when they cannot tolerate it any longer. Comparatively, there is more domestic violence these days in spite of the fact that there are less extended families these days. Actually in-laws in extended families can play dual roles. They can fan the marital discord as well as they can cement the relationships between the young couple.

Narrative 3

I am eighty-six now. I have lived a productive life till the age of 60 years. But when I lost my husband I got into depression. I feel since then I have been just surviving without any zest for life. May be this is due to my personality traits. If I look back I had an active young life after marriage. I did not go to school in my childhood. We lived in a village. At that time villages had no school either for girls or boys. Still I remember only boys were sent to nearby town's school. Some of them would walk or bike. I learnt to read and write, and do simple Maths at home, sometimes being taught by my male cousins. This skill is very handy to me in life and I believe every girl should have been taught the same at that time. I have developed this skill into a good past time. Moreover, even reading has increased my awareness and knowledge about many things around me. Though books always interested me but I was very fond of cooking and managing the home. I spent most of my time doing that in spite of the fact that I had domestic help for that.

I loved socializing with men and women in clubs and socials, and playing indoor table games. My husband never objected to that. In fact there were no social restrictions in our upper strata. But in the same geo areas of collieries; the lower strata women would not intermix with men. They were illiterate and undernourished. They were poorly treated by their men folks and often beaten by their drunken husbands. Their lives were so different from us in all respects. We had all comforts and luxuries. They had to toil very hard even to survive.

I never played any active outdoor sports but liked my walks in the house compound. We had access to fairly good medical system. There were only male doctors even for treating gynecological problems. Women did not like to be treated by male doctors but they had no option. Not many women doctors were available.

I have three daughters and no sons. But that is all right. I never craved for a son. My daughters take care of me whenever I need them. My husband had provided well for me—a residential house and enough money to live by. I was never involved in any of these planning. Neither my husband encouraged me nor I showed any inclination to do so. I took many things for granted. If I think back now, that was not a good way of handling life. Women should always be actively involved in all matters, then they are able to handle better when the other partner dies. Otherwise they are dependent. They can be miserable if their children are not good, if they are greedy, and maltreat them.

My mother became widow when she was just eighteen years old and I was only one year old. She was very beautiful.

My mother and me lived with our maternal uncles. Both of us were well provided by them. My mother had no money, no education, and no skills to earn her living. Even otherwise too she would not have been allowed to live on her own. Since she had no parents, her brothers supported her without any grudge. At least those days family support system was very good and there was lot of family integrity. I was too young to know what sort of life she would have longed for, or suffered. She married too young and became young widow. This only shows the repercussions of child or teen marriages, age gap between the marriage partners, and the low life span. She died at the age of 100+ years.

Even in her later lifetime she was very energetic, social, and full of life. Though she never expressed it but I am sure she would have missed a lot in life, being widow at 18, left with a year old child, no assets of her own and dependent on others. I think it is lot of sacrifice as well cruelty not to have remarried such young widow and deprive her of fullness of human life. But those days society never sanctioned widow remarriage at any age. When I became widow at 60+; my not remarrying was understandable. I had lived full life with my husband, had grown up children, in spite of the fact that I was not earning, I was provided well by my deceased husband and had something to fall on. I did not have to depend on my children or to live with any one. I was independent in decision about my own life.

When I got married at sixteen and moved to a city. My mother moved with me and made her home with me. Normally in our cultures, mothers do not move with married daughters. But this was an exceptional case. Firstly, my uncles were ready to support only till that time. Secondly, my husband did not mind her moving with us. In fact, he was very good to her throughout. Thirdly, since he had no parents of his own, it was easier to let her live with us; otherwise in-laws problems would have occurred and he and me had to have more allegiance towards them.

After my husband's death I just withdrew to myself. I thought that at 60 plus I was getting too old for many of the social activities. I felt I am old and I should just stay at home, supervise house chores, read, watch television, or do nothing at times. But when I look at my daughters, who are now 60+, they do not think they are old or weak or should just stay at home. For them, the concept of old age has changed. Rather with aging they seem to be having a new refreshed look about many things in life. They enjoy many different kinds of activities which earlier they were not able to get involved; because they had no leisure time, or they had children's responsibilities, or they did not had enough cash to spend.

My daughters are highly educated. But they never wanted to work after marriage; though they did work as teachers for couple of years before marriage. Their husbands never objected to their working. They were free to choose whatever they wanted to do. They chose to look after home, husband, and children rather than to work. But now at this age they want to have outside profession. Their children have settled in life, household involvement is less, domestic help is in plenty. Really, they feel bored doing nothing and also feel very unproductive when they compare themselves to the younger generations who are into so many activities. I do not think my generation ever felt that way. We would rather thank God for doing our duty well for the family, just sit back and relax. At least my daughters feel energetic to get involved into many community services which itself is quite satisfying to them.

But my grand-daughters are a different generation. Since they are educated so they must work, they must earn, and share the family expenses whether there is need or not. The argument is why should only husband work and carry all the burden. These women equally expect their husbands to share bringing up children, house management, cooking and cleaning dishes even. That is real sharing of life. They are of the opinion that with two persons equally sharing, the household management does not need all their physical and mental energies. These energies must be diverted to more fuller and productive occupations. They find the twin roles of a home-maker and career quite challenging. They are ready to accept that too. They do not want to give up their careers even if it means temporary separation from the husbands. Since they feel careers give meaning to their life, make them productive, and useful member of the society. Economic independence gives them empowerment in society, and a developed maturity.

They do enjoy shared life with husbands, look after children and home well, participate in community life, and lead an active social life. They love these demanding multi-roles and the fast pace of life. I do not think I could cope up with such pace of life. Even my daughters never led that kind of hectic life.

One of my grand-daughters had divorced just after a few months of marriage. Since both of them felt they were incompatible. They mutually decided to separate. Their argument is, there is no idea drifting in marriage, if you cannot pull on—just separate. One must live meaningfully. They had married of their own choice, family had not arranged it. They did go steady for a while. Perhaps after marriage they could not face the realities of life together. They have separated and may remarry whenever they chose. These days there is no stigma to divorce, remarriage, or even staying single, and living on her own. I think she can take this sort of decision at this point of time, because she can take care of herself economically, psychologically, and socially.

While I shudder to think what would have become of my mother and me if my uncles had not chosen to take care of us. Even in those days in many families where such considerations were not shown women were miserable, they committed suicides, they were sexually exploited, and were even lured to prostitution. But those days society was so different and women had no place in it. I am glad it has changed for better; and women on the whole have better and dignified social status.

As for my present life, I am glad that radio, TV, video, newspapers, books, and telephones at home let women like me pass time; and relax in the privacy of their homes. At the same time they have connectivity with the outside world.

There is a generational change from my mother's time to my grand-daughter's time. The outlooks, aspirations, ways of handling life, modes of dress, and even eating styles have changed. The global influences, social activism, and restlessness of women themselves have changed them for better. I am glad younger generation has been achieving what they have been striving for. Still we cannot deny the ills of society for women these days. The ugly situations of dowry demands leading to bride burning (at least Sati, burning alive of women with the dead husband is no longer practiced); domestic violence, and many crimes against women like rape etc. still occur even in upper strata of society. Women have suffered in past due to these but I feel the magnitude is more in modern times.

The big question is—Is it that men still cannot tolerate women going ahead and commit crimes against them and thus expressing their sadistic pleasure?

Narrative 4

I am quite independent and likes to be so. I am eighty-seven years. In my early years I had the advantage of education, good health, and economic independence. In my times men used to predominate taking care of the outside and business matters and we women were quite empowered to decide about household matters within the house though providing money for the same was the sole responsibility of the head of the family. We had say about upbringing the children but their educational pursuits and extra curricular activities were mainly decided by the men.

Women in my family were quite enterprising and perhaps one time they used to help the men folk in taking care of the family business. But all this was taken care of from within the homes. They never liked to move out of the house to work. Their involvement was more out of interest and desire to be productive rather than for earning money. I myself along with other women family and friends used to enjoy participating in community services for women and children, or raising funds for charities. Our usual daily pastimes was indoor recreation. We kept ourselves busy in doing beautiful arts and crafts work, embroidery, cooking sessions, reading and writing, and at times playing cards and Mahjong. I feel we were thus gainfully occupied. Since we had enough time on hand, we used to enjoy family gossiping and intrigues.

We could take walks in our lawns and I think that was the only physical exercise we indulged in. We did not have the opportunity to participate in outdoor sports like tennis, badminton, swimming etc. Though these used to be favourite pastime with the men folks and the younger generations as they were growing up. But some how we kept ourselves fit.

Since ours was a large family all living close by; we had lot of socialization among the family—the festivals, rituals, and family social functions. It was all fun and we were never bored. Rather at this point of my life I get bored and lonely at times as every one in the family is busy in their own pursuits; and less and less time is being spent in group socialization and pursuits. Moreover, families have become smaller also with children moving away from homes either by marriages or by professions.

In my younger years I enjoyed my life and I am quite relaxed with life. But the younger generations of my daughters and grand-daughters are not that relaxed. They are always in hurry to get things done, and they are tense for nothing. I think because of these tensions they never enjoy life fully and create more self-problems.

I have both daughters and sons. I think both are essential for balanced life. Still you need sons to take care of you. I like being pampered by my sons and grandsons. I am not against women inheriting family assets; but personally I would leave my assets to my sons. The main reason being that this way it stays in the family itself and in turn their sons can inherit these. But if these are given to daughters, the assets get divided and sub-divided. But if any time my daughters are in financial need, I would certainly leave property and money to them and that will be fair.

People have small families these days. It is necessary because of country's overpopulation problem. Moreover, people are also able to plan their families in a healthy way as family planning devices are easily and inexpensively available. Personally, I am in favour of having 4-6 children if one can afford it. More children gives you family stability, integration and also old age security. Imagine you have only one child and he is good for nothing or he passes away when you are still living.

My daughters' generation have still better opportunities for career, education, and marriage choices. I think they gained more from parental experiences and encouragement, ongoing process of social change, travel, and tourism. Moreover, they had the advantage of media exposure of radio, print, television, video, audio and so many other technological educational-entertainment gimmicks. They learn not only about their own country and culture, but they are exposed to diversity of cultures and their influences. They shape and lead their lives according to these cultural influences. In our times the media exposure was low. We had comparatively less awareness and knowledge of happenings around us; so our lifestyles were less influenced by extraneous influences. Rather the inter-personal influence of family and friends, peers, and teachers was predominant in shaping us.

Now-a-days women have more freedom of outdoor movements. They travel on their own. They are exposed to diversity of lifestyles. They get more opportunities to participate in outdoor sports of tennis, badminton, swimming, trekking etc. They can learn and perform arts, crafts, dance, and music without any social restrictions. In our times, women were not encouraged to learn music and dance. In rare cases if women happened to learn, they could never perform in family groups or in public. Music and dance were supposed to be courtesans' pursuits and not meant for respectable women. But at present there is no social stigma. In fact women excel in both eastern and western styles of music and dance. They give public performances for national and international audiences.

My daughter's generation is still quite conventional in their values and lifestyles. They have respect and tolerance for my generation and its lifestyles. My grand-daughters and grand-daughter-in-laws are different in their approach to life. They are not so conventional. Each one is so self-centred in pursuit of self-identity that they are least bothered about interacting with their kith and kin though they are in the same society. They bring up and educate children differently, giving them more independence, urge for creativity, outside exposure to multimedia, travel, and opportunities to interact with diversified group of people. I like it. It is a healthy trend.

They share their lives with husbands and children. They themselves are not sitting at home types (though they may not need to earn money). According to personal tastes, interests and choices they love to work and enjoy it. They thus interact with outside groups—both social and professional, and with like minded people. Whereas my daughters and me mainly like to interact with familiar groups of family and friends. May be our perspective towards life is not that balanced as that of the younger generations of today. These days they like the multi-roles and its challenges. They enjoy the tensions—what is this life if not full of care and tensions!! Compare to us, this generation has more economic, social and political awareness, participation, and empowerment.

Contentment and happiness are relative terms. Each generation is happy in its own way, each solves the problems in its own way. But still there is gradual and definite change in women's lots. Change is more noticeable among lower socio-economic strata of the society that were deprived and downtrodden. Women have benefited from development programmes initiated by the government policies after India won political freedom in 1947. British influence in India, and male activists of early 20th century were greatly responsible for reforms in women's education, banning early and child marriages, banning Sati and inhuman torturing of widows etc. The social and legislative development efforts of 50's onwards consistently brought change in women's life. The credit also goes to the women themselves who were restless as well ready to accept such change!

Narrative 5

I am 75 years. I have enjoyed the freedom, independence, and socializing in the society at all levels with male counterparts. I attribute my life's overall happiness to few factors.

As a young woman I had the freedom of education. So I had college education though few went to college at that time, I had career choice and I opted for political journalism. I married a person of my own choice. My parents did not object as my husband is a very fine person. But initially I was not accepted by my in-laws warmly. Their objections were that I belonged to another community, I was educated, and I was working in an area alien for women. I was unconventional in my behaviour, attitudes, and beliefs. And over and above, it was not an arranged marriage. Moreover, their behaviour to me was so shocking that when I entered the house as an unwelcome bride I had lock jaw and could not talk for many days!!

Henceforth, I could never live with my extended family as our ways were so different. Though in later life we mutually accepted each other.

My husband and me had good understanding with each other. He had encouraged me to gain my self-identity, my intellectual stimulation, and freedom. Our mutual understanding brought contentment and happiness to both of us in spite of struggling hard to achieve what we wanted—name and fame. We did achieve those by and by.

My spiritualism, social devotion, and such values of life as being straightforward, honest, and truthful to myself had given me impetus for better life.

I missed in life the acceptance by my in-laws' family for practicing alien values by their standards. My mother-in-law expected me to be confined to home and kitchen alone; and not to be an equal sharer with my husband in his work and social pursuits. I had been a good homemaker, interior decorator, and an excellent cook but I refused to be tied down to home alone. I wanted a different role for myself than that. I shared the 'outside world' with my husband and that had given me ultimate happiness and strength.

I have one daughter. She is young. Her generation is so different. Young women these days are self-centred, materialistic, and have less respect for human and social values. They have different life profile. The good point is she is accepted by her in-laws. If I look back, the difference in her and her in-laws may be the same but her mother-in-law generation (who is close to my generation) are more tolerant, and non-interfering. My daughter's generation willingly accept the multi-roles of life such as that of homemaker, working women, good mother, and sharer with husband in his social and professional pursuits. She brings up her children well but according to her own rearing practices. She will not listen to my suggestions. They are all outdated.

I had my own religious convictions and practices. I believe, to be a good person is being religious. It is rather hypocrisy to go on saying prayers, visit temples, and yet be dishonest in life. I am glad the younger generation also believes in such righteousness. In fact, they are not hypocrites as most of my generation is. To my generation, the religious festivals are important to give focus and direction to life at intervals. Generation previous to me looked forward to these festivals to get away from the cloistered home environments and social inhibitions thus imposed. But today's young generation follows some of these as social rituals to get together, keeping religious fasts more for physical fitness. The visit to holy places is not so much for pilgrimage as more for tourist interest and to enjoy the religious sanctity in true spirit.

Narrative 6

I am in my eighties. Destiny has not favoured me. My husband passed away when he was in his 50's. I had a young son and a daughter. Both were not ready to take care of themselves or me. Somehow I managed with the two children. I was not educated enough to earn my living. I had to manage with the savings that my husband had left and with my widow pension. In few years, both the children finished their studies and started earning. Then things became easier for me and the life was resettled.

Both my daughter and son married persons of their own choice. I did not object to it, they were fine choices. Even if I had objected, I am sure they would not have bothered about my opinion and would have done what they wanted to do. I was being looked after well by my son and daughter-in-law but God willed it otherwise.

I suffered the shock again. My son died at the young age of 40 leaving behind a young son and young widow. These two deaths had tremendous impact on my life. I was disillusioned with life. Women have to suffer the loneliness, isolation, and social deprivations without male protection in this cruel society. Further, my generation women had to even suffer the economic hardships when the earning male member expired; as those women were not trained for earning. But my daughter-in-law is in a better economic position since she is a career woman and earns well. I live with her and she is able to take good care of me both financially and emotionally. She is very understanding and we share our sorrows with each other.

My grandson is growing up well as his mother disciplined him well. She is taking good care of his education. Being highly educated women; she is able to take decisions for his educational and career choices. Whereas I could not do the same for my children; as neither I was educated, nor I had much exposure to the outside world. They had to decide for themselves.

In present times, there are no longer any social indignities for widows as it used to be in earlier times. Widows have social status these days. Widows can remarry these days both legally as well of their own choice. But neither my daughter-in-law nor me could have remarried because we had grown up children and responsibility to bring them up. Yet we have to be very cautious about the kind of life we lead so that nobody could talk ill about our reputation and cast slur on us. Not only such a thing would make our lives miserable but it will also mar the future of our children. Luckily, we have our own residential house; my son could build it in his lifetime. Otherwise nobody rents house to unattached women—whether widow or divorced; however financially well off they may be. The hesitancy is due to lack of male protection. I still remember how difficult it was for me to rent a house. Only a relative of mine rented a portion of his house to me very reluctantly and on compassionate grounds!

My childhood was comfortable. I was not sent to school but my brothers had gone. I learnt reading and writing at home. Either my brothers or my father would teach me. My mother did not even know that much. My other sisters did not learn, as they were not interested. As young girls we led sheltered life, we were not allowed to go out of the house unescorted. At home we were taught to take care of the house, cook, sew, and even look after children. In fact, in those days a girl of fifteen would be the young mother and she would be really trained for that.

My husband was quite educated. But he neither objected nor encouraged my learning more than I had. We were contented family. We as parents did aspire for high professional education for our children including our daughter and were never against our daughter pursuing a career.

My daughter works even now after marriage and children, and my daughter-in-law was working even when her husband was alive. In fact that has given her confidence to face life and its problems. I compare my life as a widow with hers: I was totally at loss but she has taken life as a challenge.

These days young women are into many things. Education and careerwise they have wider choices; and they are exposed to current global situation and influences. So their perspective of life is amalgamation of all. These days there is much less gender bias in spheres where women move. In our younger days, there was total gender discrimination in the sense that certain areas were totally tabooed to women; such as school education, professional education, employment in different disciplines, and more so in corporate offices, outdoor sports, theater, dance and music-performances and entertainment, fashion modeling etc. Now-a-days women choose freely according to their interests.

In our times women had no choice in mate selection. Family elders arranged all marriages. Marriages outside community, region, and religion were not socially approved. But these days such restrictions are less and women mostly choose or approve on their own their life partners. Even their criteria for selection are so different. They look for mental compatibility.

All said and done women have an identity today. They do face many problems and suffer but are still a happier lot. They are heard today, if they are ignored at any point, they assert to be heard. Few women participate in politics now-a-days. Indira Gandhi was our woman Prime Minister. But if more and more women would participate in politics better women policies will be made. Today, young women do suffer many other types of indignities. A decade back many young brides were burnt because of bringing insufficient dowries. In our times dowries were given more as gifts or help to set up the young couple. Mainly clothes and jewelry used to be given by the bride and bridegroom parents. In times of need her jewelry used to be her asset to fall back. Moreover, parents would give dowry according to their own financial means. Many political leaders (Indira Gandhi) took strong exception to it and through legislation banned dowry. It did control the dowry menace to some extent.

Domestic and social violence has affected women immemorial but in modern times its onslaught is worse. May be these days we are more aware of it and are concerned about it. Our Government has made legislation to protect women's rights such as marriage laws for monogamy, compulsory registration of marriages, divorce, widow remarriage, child adoption, inheritance, banning dowry, freedom to abortion without the consent of husband, and access to credit and land in the rural areas etc. These laws were necessary to give woman her rightful place in the society.

The women of today get better health care. First, they themselves are aware of the importance of good health. Second, they have access to health information, curative, and preventive measures. In my mother and grandmother's times and even in my early years, women were shy and afraid to tell any body what she was suffering from. She was not allowed to consult any male doctor; and not many women doctors were accessible. Midwife would deliver babies at homes, and treat any gynecological problems. Many women used to die in complicated childbirth or of other illness. For other minor illnesses they depended on home made herbal medicines both for themselves and for children. Those medicines used to be effective.

The religious connotations have changed with changing times. Young women of today do not visit temples daily for practical reasons. There are women who believe in being good and doing charity work or donating for charity. I believe in being good and saying my prayers at home. I go to temple or fast as a festival ritual only. My mother and grandmother believed in religious rituals, saying prayers, and reading scriptures for many hours as moral duty. I believe they were doing it as a past time too since they had less to occupy themselves at home. They did not have the freedom to visit temples as and when they chose. On festival days they could go with male escorts only.

Generations of women have developed by learning lessons from previous generations, out of practical necessity, from concerns of national and international communities, and by women themselves to create contexts to develop. Of course we cannot deny the role of the media in creating diverse and useful contexts for women to grow.

FOURTH GENERATION WOMEN

Group 2: Sixty Plus Age Group, Middle Class Socio-Economic Status

> *Eve teasing was the worst social crime against women in this generation. It was very humiliating. An unescorted woman was looked down upon as sex object only. I remember, when I would be returning home from my evening college classes it would be dark. I had to take a long route to reach home to avoid a small deserted lane that was short cut to my home. I was always afraid that some man might be just hiding there on cycle or otherwise to push me down, pull my veil, throw beetle juice on my dress, or touch me or talk dirty.*

Narrative 7

Four generations of women at the age of fourteen dreamt of diverse things. Their birth time period made the major difference.

When I was fourteen I looked forward to so many 'achievements'—such as warm and close family relationships, a good and professional education, professional career, a marriage not thrust upon me (but only when I would be ready to marry a person of my choice), and over and above opportunities for social and political participation. Divisions of society through caste and creed use to bother me and I used to feel sad at the untouchability of the menials. Public humiliation of women used to hurt me. Most often I dreamt of doing something about these social problems. This girl of 14 could do so later in her life as she was experiencing the freedom to grow.

The foremost thoughts at my mother's mind at fourteen were—would I ever have deliverance from the stifling, over-sheltered environments of my home and society? Would compulsory marriage at fourteen lead to good and changed future life? Over and above, would I face fewer constraints in life as compared to my mother?

My grandmother at fourteen perhaps already married and pregnant could not think of a world existing beyond the inner walls of home and family. A helpless, powerless person with no self-identity, no outside exposure to any information. Awareness of anything was just not there. She did not have the freedom to grow! Her main thought would have been—should women be born in this society?

So these were the three generations of mother, grandmother and me. But the present 'transformed generation' of my daughter have certainly grown up differently at fourteen. The wide opportunities given by parents, afforded by environments, access to education, global media exposures have created lot more awareness, information, knowledge about many matters such as society, health, science, arts, and politics. They have the freedom to grow in many directions!

Thus four generations had different experiences and encounters with life.

I grew up in an environment of gender segregation rather than discriminations. Things were opening for women. There were separate girls schools and colleges; and only female teachers were teaching girls. Women were only opting for social science subjects. Science and engineering, medical subjects were being reserved for males only. Women doctors were only trained for gynecology, and training facilities were opening up for women paramedical. Wherever women were working in public offices (which was quite rare, it has just started) there were ladies lunchrooms. There would be reserved seats for ladies in public transport, cinema houses, and even in restaurants. There would be separate ladies queues. Such was the segregation scenario. I do not know whether it was to protect women against males, or to show them respect, or to let them grow for a while without the stifling domination of males. I think if third was true, it did work.

Gradually, as I was growing up, in sixties, the segregation scenario did transform into co-educational system. Both male and female teachers were teaching in the co-educational system.

More and more women were being trained for science and engineering professions. Women were getting out of the female only professions and were trying to get into the male dominated professions. Earlier there was gender discrimination in educational areas, but now the discrimination shifted to the work place where men and women were working together. Women of my generation had hard time making their niche. Gradually, ladies did not need reservation in social domain to grow but surely they were demanding equality, and reservations in professions. At early stages males only doled out such jobs as clerks and secretaries in corporate and government offices. Any front office jobs such as in post offices, banks, airlines, restaurants and hotels etc. were not socially approved for women as there were more public dealings and visibility. With lots of hardships they graduated to the middle level jobs. Currently, women head many high-ranking jobs in industries, corporate and government offices both in management and technical fields.

Mine was 'transition generation'. Since this was the transition period when woman was graduating to have access to education in different disciplines, careers, professions, and struggle for freedom of movements for her self-identity in order to be respected as a human being and not humiliated as a sex object.

She was demanding freedom to choose her marital lifestyle—when to marry and whom to marry or to remain single even. Parents and guardians were encouraging marriages as facilitator, and these were not arranged as were done in early generations. Still women had to marry though at a higher age, and she had to abide by regional and religion restrictions only whereas the earlier generations had to follow the caste and community restrictions in addition.

Generation of today has gone a step further. They can remain single if they choose, can go steady, and marry the person of their own choice without any caste, community, and regional restrictions. Still inter-religion marriages are socially disapproved.

Political Will was in favour of developing my generation of women and legal protection was given to women by new laws for marriage (banning of child marriages and bigamy, freedom to marry when adult, compulsory registration of marriages, widow remarriage, divorce, dowry etc.), protect women against domestic and social violence, inheritance, equality in education and employment. She asserted her human dignity in making decisions for herself. Though there was legal protection in these respects, still lots of social efforts were needed to give women the right place. For example, she had the right to divorce or a widow could remarry. Still lot of social stigma was attached to these practices; therefore women were reluctant to take steps in these directions. But these days there is more openness about these matters.

As I was growing up I faced more gender discrimination in social interactions. In fact, free mixing with males without being chaperoned was socially disapproved. So much so that a lone woman mixing with men or working with them, or even seen alone with a man publicly would be labelled as woman of loose morals. Men would be thus hypocritical in their attitudes towards women.

Women had to face lot of eve teasing when moving alone or unescorted. Quite likely, the freedom of women, their coming out of veils was not acceptable to many men, they would behave badly towards them and humiliate them. Women had to struggle hard, were assertive, and aggressive to preserve the newly won freedom. At one point of time the magnitude of eve teasing was so great that police had to patrol strategic points, and teasers were arrested and punished. These deterrent measures did check this shameful menace to some extent.

The younger generation of women today does not have to face these humilities anymore. The attitude and behaviour of younger generation of males have changed through healthy intermixing of the sexes. They themselves resent this atrocious and shameful behaviour.

In my times women were discriminated in work place. They were not assigned responsible jobs, or involved in policy decisions, or for being considered for promotions. Since women were considered as secondary earner (though that may not be the family reality always) who was usurping one male earner, less intelligent, and less capable of handling responsible jobs. These attitudes have undergone change for the present generation.

My generation decades were fast changing times for women development. Every decade brought substantial change in women's life. The decade of 50's to 60's was great for women education, employment, social, and legal protection. New vistas were opening for women in professions and lifestyle in 70's and 80's. The decades of 80's and 90's are more all-round achievement oriented.

Religion for me is a way of life focusing on good values and God. I am not fatalistic, but I do believe that whatever has to happen will happen. One has to reap for the past Karma (deeds). Attitudes towards religion has changed across generations. Earlier generations believed in religious myths, stereotypes, and rigid ritualistic practices. My grandma believed in reading holy books and observing religious rituals and fasts. She was very fatalistic in attitude and behaviour. My mother believed in saying her daily prayers at home with occasional visits to temples and religious gatherings; and practicing rituals in moderate. She was fatalistic in attitude but not so much in behaviour. She would believe in horoscope reading by astrologer but would not practice those readings. Generation of today believe in good values, social charity, and philosophizing about religion/s.

The transition generation was moving ahead, trying to achieve equality, and social justice.

When my mother was young, she dreamt of reading a lot and being highly educated, and a doctor of medicine! This was the beginning of 20th century in India. Women lived behind the veils (Purdah), were not allowed to leave the four walls of the house. If at all they had to go out, they must travel with a male escort and in the curtained carriages. Women from respectable families were not allowed to walk on the street. They had to be protected from male glances. Only women prostitutes could walk the street at dusk only. Such was the mobility given to women, which made their life almost immobile. In the buggy (horse drawn carriage) several young eyes (of girls) would peek and get the glimpse of the outside world, a yearning to walk on the streets on their little feet, inhale fresh, and free air. Those were innocent wishes though never granted by the cruel society of those days.

It was stifling to remain indoor most of the times. No playgrounds, no playmates, no exposure to world around. What a life for young girls? They had only to wait for 'marriage' which might be for better or worse. They would be married at the age of 14 or 15 years. Early marriages meant a few more happenings in the girls' lives. An end of day dreaming and facing the practicalities of life. It was a period of making efforts towards adjusting to in-laws family, with the likely possibility of her being accepted or rejected by them; which in turn could make her life happy or unhappy. She had no financial independence because quite likely even the husband himself would be dependent on his family. The syndrome of the extended family with the mother in-law's harsh treatment could occur. She would force herself to accept the in-laws family and wean herself from the birth family. After marriage due to other constraints, there would be less likelihood of any interaction with the parental families. The means of transport were also not that easy those days and travelling was not safe for women. It was also not customary to visit parental family.

Early marriages could also mean early start and long periods of reproduction, thus raising large families. Those days there were no birth control devices to plan families.

As a dream unfulfilled, my mother wanted her daughters to be highly educated and professionals. She could never go to school because of Purdah system. There were no girls school, no female teachers. Boys were sent to schools and colleges for both general and professional education. They were even sent abroad to qualify further. Whereas the women were not even given the opportunity to read and write.

My mother longed to read and write. She had flair for languages. Her family had money to spent. She coaxed her mother to let her study at home. Her mother herself had never been to school or be educated. She wanted to help her, but she had no voice in decision-making about her children's education or future. She pleaded with the male relative in-charge (she was a widow) to let my mother study at home.

An old Maulvi (Muslim priest), and an elderly Hindu priest were engaged to teach Hindi, Urdu, and Persian languages to the three sisters including my mother. They had to sit behind the curtain to learn. Even against these odds my mother learnt as she was enthusiastic but the other two only played; and teachers had no way to control them. My mother fulfilled her dreams through educating her daughters well. She was always in favour of women's learning and she inspired her daughters to achieve high.

Times changed, there was change in Indian society for women. Many factors contributed to it. The predominant was British influence in India. British objectively assessed the sad plight of Indian women in general with constraints of education, freedom of safe movements, domestic and social violence of killing newborn daughters, Sati i.e. burning widow alive on the husband's pyre, Devdasis (temple dancers—a kind of prostitution) and so on. This created awareness and efforts of Indian women and men activists to cooperate with the government and start the process of change. Such initiatives brought betterment of women in many directions of life.

Many women's life including my mother's life was swayed by this change. Upto the age of 14 she led a constrained life. But marriage at that age to an educated person and the opportunity to live in the open environment of New Delhi, where even the British influence was quite predominant changed her life. Her husband was young though only 10 years her senior.

Living in New Delhi, she experienced different lifestyle. It was growing up in interesting environments. On one hand, New Delhi was exposing her to the openness of British society and its changed ways of living; and on the other hand the young brides were migrating to New Delhi along with their husbands from their own parental close society. This group of women were easily and readily susceptible to change. She had freedom of movement, dress, and socially mixing with other neighbours, friends and even males. There was no social taboo to accompany her husband to social parties, movies, restaurants, or even for walks. This was a good change for her; and she matured and developed confidence in herself. Of course, it was too late for her to go to school. Girls' schools were opening, and she could visualize education for her daughters.

Early marriage and non-availability of birth control devices those days meant children being born too soon after marriage. It also meant raising on an average a large family of six to eleven live children excluding miscarriages. My mother had seven children though she never wanted more than two children. There was no way to escape the large family.

She felt quality of life suffered as more and more children were born, and finances constrain. Her health too suffered in the process. Those days babies were delivered at home by semi-trained midwife; many women even use to die in childbirth due to complications. Public hospitals were just coming up with small gynecological departments to treat women's gynecological problems. Medical colleges were opening to train women doctors. In 40's only negligible number of women doctors were in Delhi. These were the young women doctors who had struggled hard to train themselves against all social odds. They belonged to few pioneering families. Awareness was being built for both preventive and curative measures about women's health; among women as well male members of the society. More than women themselves, men were the decision-makers about women's health programmes.

My mother was the dominating figure in our family. My father encouraged her to learn and take care of family matters outside the home. He used to cooperate with her. This encouraged family sharedness that she had missed while growing up in her parental home. Since she missed closeness with her mother due to her being helpless and non-assertive; she was very close to her own children and demonstrated lot of care and affection for them. Taking a leaf from her own life, that was her firm belief, give a woman freedom, encouragement, and the right ambience; and she would be the most useful member of society.

I remember my maternal grandmother as very beautiful with long black hair. She became widow at the age of 21 years. Her husband was thirty years older than her. He married her when she was only 14 years. This was his second marriage since he had no children from the first wife. My grandfather died young (though people use to live long those days) leaving behind four very young children—three daughters and a son. The oldest girl was only five. He left lot of money and residential house. Imagine those days life for such women with no formal education and skills to earn, no empowerment for decision-making for herself, her children, and no access to manage her own money. Everything had to be supervised by a male member of her husband's family.

She was helpless, dependent on male relatives to take care of her needs and life in general. What about her own self-identity, her dreams, and her ambitions for herself? Probably they died a natural death with her childhood. I remember my grandma achieving her self-hood probably by submerging herself in reading holy scriptures from dawn to dusk which preached 'detachment' from the worldly ties. She tried to detach herself from her children and the world around her. Whether she succeeded or not, but it surely was a strong effort to sublimate her life over which she has no control. At 21 when life had just bloomed, she started withering by the cruel controls of the world around her; which constrained her natural blossoming as a human being.

Imagine the conflicts in her mind. She wanted to run around, be frolicsome, and enjoy life. But she was doomed to abstain from all, starve her body, read scriptures only from dawn to dusk whether she understood them or not! She wanted to take solace in taking care of her children but she was helpless and not empowered. So she feigned to be emotionally detached from them.

She was cooped in the house with other female members and children of the extended family who would live in the main house. Men quarters would be away from the main house. Women quarters used to be in big havelis. These havelis would have inside open courtyards or terraces where women could sit and move about for fresh air. Otherwise they were not allowed to go out of the house.

Women would keep themselves busy in the household chores, doing beautiful embroidery and artwork, developing culinary art of making pickles in large quantities to be distributed among relatives. They would not do the daily cooking. Special male cooks who had to observe lot of kitchen hygiene and personal cleanliness always handled daily cooking. Women of the house would not be allowed to interfere in any food planning or marketing. Male members would take care of that. They would not do any marketing for kitchen or for their daily requirements. But for her clothing and jewelry, the travelling salesmen would come to the house for selection of merchandise. These salesmen had to be old and trustworthy and from reliable referenced shops.

Occasionally these women would go escorted in veiled carriages for temple visits on festivals and family ritual days. They might visit the house of a local close relative for 13 days on the death in that family. Women were not allowed to participate in public functions on such occasions as to accompany the funeral or a bridegroom procession. They would observe rituals at home only.

My grandma had no real friends. Women were not allowed any social visits from local or out of station women community members. Women could meet other women from their community clans and relatives on festivals, religious rituals, weddings, and deaths. Those were the only times when they could enjoy meeting others. Since no regular social visits or get together were allowed, even no telephones connecting them, there was very little chance for real friendships to develop.

It is hard to imagine how my grandma or women in those days passed their daily life with so many constraints and not many facilities available. Awareness and knowledge about world, national, regional, or even local matters were out of bounds for them because there were no television, radio was just developing, newspapers and other print media was not widely circulated. My grandma had no media exposure. She had her holy books in her native language to read. As postal facilities had developed she could write to her daughters when they were married away and thus express herself.

She relied mainly on interpersonal communication channels for expressing herself but with whom? My grandma could chat with her mother-in-law, her daughter-in-law a teenager, and the babies around. Her only son was not that close to her. Every morning and evening dutifully he would check how she was doing, did she need anything and that was all. No real closeness or sharedness.

With the passage of time her daughters got settled, grandchildren were born. Every year she would look forward to the visits of married daughters and grandchildren for 2-3 months summer vacations. Then the house would be alive with all the activities. I could see glow of happiness on her face when her kith and kin were around her. These small joys she missed when she grew up. She could never visit her parental family alone or with her children as it was not customary those days. She was glad the times had changed. At least now she could enjoy her children and grandchildren's visits.

All said and done she led a lonely life but she was no exception; that was the life for all women. Loneliness, low family sharedness, and nothing to look forward in life except drudgery; that was the life they had to lead. These women never had the will to live long. They would start withering at the age of fifty; feeling physically and mentally old, and would soon fade away. My grandmother died when she was sixty. I still feel if she had not suffered the constraints of life she would have lived longer!

Narrative 8

In my younger days I was very enthusiastic about participating in cultural activities and it was lot of fun. I enjoyed my college days. We had discipline and limited freedom in college, we respected our teachers and utilized our time in academics and healthy extracurricular activities. But these days students are so much into violent and politically motivated activities that they lose interest in their academic pursuits.

These days younger generation of women do work hard in academics but they are superficial in their attitudes towards, work, play, and relationships. All the time they are in the rat race of competitions and have very little time to enjoy life and their achievements in peace. Whereas our generation enjoyed life, no rush-rush, even the little coffee sessions with colleagues meant joy and relaxation.

Our mothers' generation never got the opportunity to enjoy freedom of thought and expression, of going out on their own, getting educated in schools, and for careers. Over and above they had no economic independence. They had little exposure to the outside world through media or otherwise. But still they were contented in the confines of their homes and in the folds of their families. But there was definitely an underlying and undefined restlessness about not able to do activities that their male counterparts were doing—especially independence to shape their own lives, self-identity, and empowerment. In those days some of the women activists achieved it for themselves, and struggled hard to achieve them for women in general. The male social activists were also in the forefront to help women either because they did not like the gender discriminations or they sympathize with particular cause. It did satisfy their ego.

But our mothers' 'restlessness' created more opportunities for our generation. Education was a boon, girls could move out freely, though with certain hazards. They could be in employment if they choose and be economically independent. They have self-identity, say in shaping their own lives and that of their own children; in financial management and investments, and for better health care for self and family. The freedom and the medical technology to control reproduction of children were a saviour to them and added to their human dignity.

Some of the early credit to raise the status of women goes to British influence in India, and the efforts of Indian male social and political activists. They banned Purdah (veil system) and Sati, created infrastructure for girl's education, and health care through women doctors and paramedical. Later, after independence of the country in 1947 our own political leaders were aware of women's indignities; and they made efforts to better their lot through many development programmes and legislation. They gave social empowerment to women through change of laws of inheritance, marriage and divorce, anti-dowry, anti-Sati. They further facilitated economic empowerment through employment. Both male and female social activists contributed towards it. Our generation also benefited not only through these national efforts but also through International awareness and efforts to bring women to the mainstream development.

In the family also, one could not deny the biggest contribution of the male members of the family—father, brothers, or husbands. Since there has always been the male dominant influence which could make or mar the change. For better, the males respected the 'new woman' and were enthusiastic about her growth as equal. This was the general trend.

Our generation women had another dilemma—women making women suffer. My mother-in-law liked me but she was very dominating woman and proud of her beauty. She was very possessive of my husband (being the only son). She would always complain about me to my husband about my beauty, appearance, and independent ways and would enjoy vicarious pleasure out of it. I was tolerant of it because my husband never admonish me about it openly rather I knew he was supportive of my ways. I used to rationalize that she is envious of my generation's independent ways and husbands' giving equality, which she never enjoyed. She expressed her envy by being critical of me. But if the mothers-in-laws and daughters-in-laws have no empathy for one another; they would have strained relationships and feel miserable. The older women would blame the bad ways of the younger generation.

I myself pity my mother and mother-in-law generation. They were treated as non-entity. No wonder those days nobody wanted to beget girls and yet girls must be born to further the progeny. My grandmother's generation was still worse. In addition they had to observe Purdah, and had no social female or male interactions. They were only sex objects to their husbands to beget innumerous children. Children were very important to the males to further the dynasty.

At least in my mother's generation they could interact with family male members. There was no Purdah. She could go out with her husband wherever he chose to take her. Thus relatively she was better off and was inching towards a different status for herself. She could aspire for her daughters the same type of 'change' she was looking forward to.

My daughter and daughter-in-law's generation is so different. Actually I do not want to label these as generation gaps rather they are generational journeys and changeovers. They are more independent, confident, and know their own minds. They share full lives with their own husbands and children. They feel restless if not faced with the challenge of life and multi-roles of modern life.

I have healthy bend towards religion. There are generational changes towards religion *per se*. I look at religion as a philosophy of life to give oneself peace and contentment. I do visit temples and sit for prayers whenever I feel like. I also believe in some of the religious rituals since I believe they give you a balanced look at life. In life, the start of religious bend is around sixties usually. But younger generation of today is ready to have intellectual discussions about religion even earlier than that. Beliefs in rituals and temple visits are seen more as social interactions. They do believe in observing them more for social obligations without any compulsions. Focus is more on spiritualism rather than religious practices.

My grandmother's attitude and observation of religion was a necessary way of life, occupation, and past time. Their focus was on saying prayers at home, and reading religious books and scriptures. Since women had no media exposure and social networking to keep them busy; they devoted most of their free time to religious practices, occasional temple visits, or participating in holy gatherings. Practicing of religious rituals was compulsory. It also gave women opportunities to get out of the house and socially interact. Women looked forward to these eagerly. Festivities, music, and dance during these rituals could throw inhibitions to winds. An analysis of the religious folk songs could show the women's pinning for social and male interactions, and an urge for freedom of movements. As soon as women were married in those days (about 14-15 years), their religious practices would start. Sometimes I really wonder if these practices were really thrust upon them, or they were happy observing them, and incorporated some of the holy teachings in their lives.

Interestingly, widows in those days had to practice religion more rigorously to discipline their young minds from any sexual wanderings. Those days' women use to become widow at young age as there used to be 10 to 20 years difference between the two partners, and remarriage was considered sin. For them, the usual ritual used to be predawn cold baths, scantily dressed, observing fast, saying prayers for 2-3 hours till their mind was supposed to be commune with God and in peace with self.

Narrative 9

I have seen the ups and downs of life in diversified ways. My father allowed me to have good professional education and go for job. My brother and me were given the equal opportunities. I had the choice to marry on my own but my marriage was facilitated by my parents. I had freedom to socially interact and decide for myself what I wanted to be in life. My father and brother were the encouraging force in my early life. My mother had very little role in these matters. When my mother was raised, when she was married, begot children, there was always the male domination effect. She had no empowerment, no desire or role in decision-making, no education, and no economic independence. But I am sure somewhere in her mind must be lurking longings that her daughter should achieve what she missed in life. That is why she was always very encouraging in whatever I wanted to do.

She commanded great respect in the family and led peaceful and contented life. She married at young age of 15 years and was molded by my father and her in-laws family. She felt she belonged to this family only. I guess her premarriage life would not have been that happy, as those days young girls were confined to home only with very little freedom to go out. But marriage must have given her opportunity to get out of that environment and enjoy the freedom. She was encouraged by my father and by urban influences. She had been consistently religious—to say her prayers, observe rituals and festivals. These provided get-togethers with friends and family.

I had all the opportunities to make my life happy. I suffered exploitation, physical and mental violence by my husband and his family. I could tolerate it no longer and in the fifth year of my marriage I walked out of it. I left my young daughters with him. I could do that because I knew I could earn my living and would be able to take care of myself. But still at that point of time, society did not approve of women living all by themselves. So I returned to my parental home. My parents accepted me but they were powerless to intervene with my husband.

I did not initiate divorce though I had the legal right to do so. As divorce was social stigma on woman's life. Moreover in those days men always use to think of divorcee as easy sexual object. Later on, after few years of separation from my husband the divorce was legalized.

It is much convenient for younger generation of today to get divorce. Firstly, it has no social stigma or taboo. Secondly, the couples separate with mutual consent out of the courts. Therefore, money, time, efforts, and precious years of life are not wasted. Thirdly, there is no stigma or taboo for remarriage. They can remarry if they want to at an appropriate age, as life is not wasted seeking for divorce. Fourth, divorcee women are accepted and respected by the society as living on their own. So they do not always have to return to parental homes. The divorce rate is increasing in younger generation because of less tolerance, less compatibility, more confidence in economic empowerment, and individuality. Moreover social support along with legal sanctions have made things easier.

I could not remarry as social support was lacking. I left my two children with him as a sort of punishment. But if I look back I rather punished myself since I was devoid of children's love. I could not have more children as I did not remarry. I try to cultivate my daughters now since they are adults. But I feel there is lack of warmth in this relationship due to gap of years or the trauma they suffered in their early life. Anyway in this sordid relationship, it is the woman who suffers both ways and most. I have no regrets the way I shaped my later life. At least I had dignity, peace, and self-identity. The activating factor that changed my lifestyle was that I was not ready to be exploited by males. I was aware of my rights, social equality, and human rights.

In earlier days, in such situation, generations of my mother and grandmother would have died by being downtrodden and exploited, as they were helpless and economically dependent. But there is a social dilemma. At times I feel, those days still women commanded better respect in society in spite of the fact that they did not have much education, economic independence and empowerment, and there were no divorce or inheritance laws. Now-a-days gender equality is practiced but there is very little respect in speech, mannerism, and attitudes among the young.

My two daughters have access to diversity of education, careers, and opportunities to achieve what they wanted in life. They have chosen their own life partners.

Sometimes I find the younger generation as over-confident, and very confused. They are all the time looking for challenges, multiple roles, and proving points. They enjoy competition and are restless without it. All they look for is competition, challenges, and sharing in different walks of life.

The big question is which generation is happier? I think happiness is a relative term. All the five generations felt happy in their own way. All of them have been feeling something lacking in their previous generations or among themselves. The 'restlessness' of the generations is perhaps stimulation for life to come.

I am religious. I believe in saying daily prayers, rituals, and going on pilgrimages. I am great devout of Sai Baba. Though I do not visit temple daily. I feel being religious gives you focus for achievement, peace, and tranquillity. It gives you moral conviction. My mother and grandmother's generations were religious to the extent of being superstitious and fatalistic. I am not superstitious but I believe in astrology. But religion has no place in younger generation's life. They are not superstitious and fatalistic. They are materialistic. They observe less rituals and festivals as these have lost the old values attached to them. Moreover, in olden times these were used for social get-together (especially by women) and throwing away social inhibitions. But now women do not have to suffer those inhibitions any longer. They can create socials whenever they want. There is freedom of speech and movements.

Narrative 10

My generation has the enthusiasm and understanding of parents to educate daughters. In fact, my mother is not very educated but she is very intelligent with lots of practical sense.

She was in favour of educating us (we were two sisters), and go for office careers. My marriage was arranged by my parents' choice. I do not know whether my parents were broadminded to accept if I had any other choice. Even in those days of 60's young men and women never interacted enough to make their own marriage choices. Moreover, parents would never give them permission to go steady or interact freely with males for fear of social stigma. They were guided more by social opinion rather their own judgments in this regard.

In 50's generally parents would not discriminate between sons and daughters for education and health care; but sons were given more food, nutrition, freedom for outdoor sports and recreation, and opportunities to socialize. I was not even allowed to cycle down to college. Whereas the girls were restricted even to visit their girl friends or go unescorted anywhere. I think this was more to protect women from public sexual harassment rather than to constrain them.

There was no gender discrimination as such in the work places but our male bosses and even parents use to guide us not to interact with male colleagues in or outside the office; or even to work after normal office hours when only one or two males may be around. Male colleagues were just treated like pieces of furniture. I think that was very unprofessional way of being involved in careers. It was 50's and women have just started going for employment outside their homes. Parents and society were more concerned about sexual harassment at work place. I think it was very ridiculous. Working women also reluctantly abided by these work place restrictions as they did not want to loose their newly won freedom to work. They further restricted themselves by subdued mannerism, and sober dress etc.

Gradually, since 70's the attitude towards working women is changing. In fact whole scenario is changed. The younger generation working women are visible in varied fields. They are the bosses, they work shoulder to shoulder with their male colleagues. Their visibility is ubiquitous. They move about unescorted late in the evenings. They participate and share equally in work and work related decisions. They share aspirations, joys, sorrows with their male colleagues. Just because she is woman does not constrain her any longer.

This change has been gradual but good. Women have become more productive, and now even more choices are open to them. Women have changed their work place mannerism and dress. It is no longer subdued but appropriate for work environments.

The younger generation women—my daughter and daughter-in-law are highly educated and more career-oriented. They accept the challenges of multi-roles of career and family. They are very egoist, and self-centred with lot of self-confidence. Somehow, what I do not like about them is the lack of dignity, and respect shown to elders. Neither they can live in extended families nor they can maintain extended family relationships whereas this is the foundation of Indian families. In my times, not only we would have cordial relationships and warm welcome for our immediate in-laws and parental families but also even their distant relatives would be welcome. Now-a-days with small families (only two children), these women do not want to be burdened with any extra home care for guests. The extra time available from work and home they want to spend on recreation, socialization, and developing them (which is a new concept). They want to establish their self-identity. I personally think this should be encouraged to a moderate extent. But watching the current scenario, the limits are exceeded in the name of women lib.

I am quite happy these days women have the choice of marriage and going steady. It is accepted by the society. May be society has become wiser by seeing dowry bride-burning and violence against women. There are few caste, community, and regional restrictions for marriages. Though in our times there were rigid restrictions, marriages were arranged, girls were not allowed to go steady.

Since my generation, women's awareness, and attitude towards own health and family, food, nutrition has undergone tremendous change for quality of lifestyles. More and more health care knowledge and facilities are available, and women are making use of them in big way in order to enjoy better life. They do not want to suffer silently any more like my grandmother generation did. I shudder to think how they suffered silently. If they were sick, only home medicines were given, and often those use to heal them. It was problematic for complicated diseases. Male doctors could not examine them, as these women would be in Purdah; and there was great paucity of women doctors. Even childbirth used to be handled by midwives. Many women use to die in complicated and difficult childbirths. There was no concern about pre-natal or post-natal medical care. Birthrate was high and so was infant mortality.

It was not so much neglect about illnesses only but as far general health and nutrition was concerned; women were generally neglected. In fact, male members were given better diet and also non-vegetarian food on the plea that they had to go for work and earn. Even women themselves were not bothered about their health, fitness or body shape. They used to be married at 14-15 years, had long reproductive years, bearing several children and miscarriages without any refurbished health care. Rather they would suffer ill health, diseases, low energy, and early old age symptoms. Still in general, women used to live long. I do not know the reasons for such longevity. My grandmother died at 90 and she had never seen a doctor or been to a hospital. Apparently she looked healthy but I cannot say if there were any undiagnosed diseases. May be they lived self-disciplined lives, were more relaxed without any stress of modern life. At home they used to get all physical exercises through household chores. Now-a-days we have sedentary jobs, electronic appliances to do many of the household chores, and close apartments with low air quality. To live in houses surrounded with open lawns and greenery is a matter of past.

My grandmother used to tell me they had to create such household chores as grinding grains, washing clothes, and going up and down the stairs in big houses etc. to get physical exercises. Even those chores were not enough to maintain physical fitness. No structured programmes of physical exercises, sports, or even walks were encouraged. Most of the household chores were still sedentary whether it was cooking, washing of clothes, knitting, sewing, or even saying their prayers. Life was just existence, without enough of mental or physical stimulation and upkeep. I am sure I would have never been happy in such existence. It was waste of human life as such! But still women in those days were a happy and contented lot.

My mother too had undergone such constrains when growing up but she was glad she got married at the age of 15 years to an educated, and urbanite young person who let her grow into a wholesome life.

Modern marriage institution is stable and sharing but there is increased incompatibilities in this relationship. Divorce helps to end the hardships of marriage. Women do not drag an unsuccessful marriage. They divorce with mutual consent and restart with remarriages. There is both legal and strong social sanction for it. In my younger days marriage laws protected women but divorcee women had hardly any social status or approval. Further, double standard was practiced in this regard. It was difficult for divorcee women to get remarried though divorced men would even get married to unmarried girls. Therefore, only in extreme hardships women would opt for divorce. Economic independence through employment and inheritance laws further encouraged women to take such steps since they had something to fall back upon.

Religion is a matter of convenience and choice these days. What matter most is moral conviction, good values of life. My mother and grandmothers had the same religious philosophy but in addition they had the time and inclination to say prayers daily, visit temples and holy places, participate in religious gatherings occasionally, and give overt expression to such beliefs through rituals and festivals.

Narrative 11

I grew up in sheltered and protective environment in spite of the fact that my family is well educated and well connected. But somehow they do not trust their women. I am 60 plus now and unmarried, and so is my older sister who is 70 plus now. Both of us live with our brother and his family though they shifted to our residential house. I am educated, I have been teaching in a school for the last thirty years. I have no freedom of movements. I cannot go and interact with anybody I want to. I am constrained in my social and professional interactions because of my family's attitude. Wherever I go I must be escorted by my brother, or any male member of the family. It is so stifling at times. Same is true for my sister. So we do not have a life of our own.

My father died when I was very young. We are seven sisters and two brothers. All sisters are extremely beautiful. My mother was very beautiful also. My mother was in her forties when my father died. He has left her money but no residential house. She was neither educated nor had the skills for any kind of employment. My older sister had been married at that time. It was her husband, though a young person handled all her family affairs about finances, decision-making about my other siblings' schooling, living, marriages etc. till we all children grew up. But still my mother maintained an independent house and managed the family well.

I never found my mother helpless, frustrated, or resentful as we two sisters found ourselves these days. Though she relied on my brother-in-law for male support but she had say and authority in whatever had to be done. She had a large family—nine children and may be couple of miscarriages; but she never complained. Such was the state of women health care at that time. I really feel good when I see 1-2 children family. I hate large families.

At least if women become widows at young age; they do not have to worry about rearing large number of children till they themselves die. Moreover, sometimes with one or two children the woman can remarry also. Though in my mother's time there was neither laws nor social acceptance for widow remarriage. But widowers used to marry even unmarried women and there was social acceptance for that also. That was social hypocrisy. This was the same practice in my grandmother's times. In addition, those days widows were physically and mentally tortured by social deprivations and social taboos; such as they would not be allowed to participate in marriages, religious rituals etc. for fear of ill omen. But in my mother's time, at least widows had social status and they were not tortured socially. Of course now we are very open about widow remarriages, and there is social acceptance.

These days society is very open to women. There is no social stigma even if women remain unmarried. In earlier days it was unheard of. She had to marry even to a worthless fellow, and because of this she might suffer in life. Interestingly, when she would suffer, nobody from her parental family would protect her. They would be fatalistic about her sufferings. Thus girls were considered burden by parents. My sister and I did not marry but nobody condemns us. I think by the time I was ready for marriage my mother was tired of getting her other children married and did not have the inclination to look for a suitable match for me. I was the youngest daughter. Though I had started working but I had neither opportunity nor allowed to intermix with men to make my own choice of marriage partner. My brothers are younger than I am. They never bothered to fix my marriage. In fact both my brothers married of their own choice and in inter-community; which was not common those days. My older sister did not marry because my mother wanted somebody to rely on as she was growing old. So my sister continued to work. She could have married after her death though she was 40+ at that time. If I look back, I think both of us did not marry because of family's non-cooperation.

In fact, when my mother was alive, we three women were living together. At that time brothers were in job elsewhere. At least those days we had some self-identity. My mother was also strict about women moving unescorted. For whatever may be her experiences in life; she was keen that after her death we two sisters should live by ourselves. And that is why when she died at the age of 80 plus she left a residential house for us. So that we do not have to depend on others and be ruled by others' decisions. But that has not worked for us because the moment our mother passed away my brother shifted with us to give us sheltered life. We are grown up, are mature, earn well; but have no self-identity or assertion to act in our own way. May be both of us are not assertive enough and are exploited by our male relatives for whatever reasons. That is our weak point.

My mother though not educated, she never discriminated, but educated us well. She encouraged us all to work as teachers till some of us got married at an appropriate age. Teaching was supposed to be a conventional and respectable career for girls at that point of time. My mother never approved of any office careers for us. But my brother restrains our social mixing and even outdoor recreation activities.

I am glad I have been working. It is a coed school. I do interact with male and female teachers professionally and socially in the school only. At least I have freedom for that many hours and do not experience gender discrimination in work environments.

My mother was quite religious which meant reading holy books at home or sometimes participating in religious gatherings. That was her pastime. My sister is religious. She often goes to particular temple to do charity work and participate in religious gatherings. She says her prayers daily at home. But I am not particular about it. My religious conviction is to lead a clean life. Now-a-days religion is a matter of personal choice. Earlier, for women it was a social ascription to lead their lives in particular religious way.

Science and technology has made life comfortable for women both at grass-roots level and for those in the upper social classes. The technology used for household appliances whether electronic or otherwise has reduced the household drudgery, made life comfortable and give women more time for other pursuits in or out of the house; or even to go for a job. Even the entertainment technology such as TV, radio, VCR, have all contributed not only for entertainment, but made them aware and informed about what is happening in the world and specially about women in different cultures and countries. Further, advancement in telecommunication has made interpersonal communication far more easy and distance oriented. They can enjoy these technologies in the privacy of their home. Such an awakening is very stimulating. Technology has created many jobs for women.

My grandmother's generation has no exposure to media. Radio was just coming on the media scene but not accessible to women. Television was not there. India was producing silent films at that time but women being in Purdah had no access to cinema; nor there were cinema houses in all cities. Women had no news or information about happenings around her and no entertainment through media. All news and entertainment was only through word of mouth. There were no telephones. Since household technology was also not very advance, most of the household chores were done manually. They did not have refrigerators. Main emphasis was to buy fresh food and cook afresh. They use to cook on charcoal or wood fire. These chores used to consume most of the women's time. Hand held fans, and later in the early 19th century ceiling fans, electric light bulbs, water taps helped women to lead more relaxed life.

My grandmother would have travelled rarely. She would have travelled from her parental village to her in-laws village, just when she got married, since means of transportation were very poor. Women could travel in horse drawn buggies, bullock carts, in palanquins carried by four men. A low network of trains had just started in the last decade of 18th century. Neither it was safe for women to travel nor they were encouraged to do so. Women travel was only localized; she would not even visit her parental family for all her life what to talk about sightseeing trips! Such was the hardship.

But by my mother's time transportation means have improved. In early 1900, there was better network of trains, and few cars, and buses could be seen around. Travelling was comparatively safe. Women were not frequent travellers but they would travel to relatives and for other family social occasions. But still travelling for sightseeing was unheard of. In 50's radio in homes and access to films in cinema houses created entertainment channels for women. Television and VCR were available in 70's for education, information, and entertainment. In 60's onwards the focus was on developing or making accessible household technology for women. The coal and the woodfire was replaced by kerosene oil stove and later cooking gas cylinders were available in bigger cities. By 70's refrigerator has become a necessity.

There was boom in household technology in 80's. Refrigerator, washing machines, ovens, microwaves, toasters, grinder-mixers, air-coolers, air-conditioners, and telephones etc. have become necessity for life. These have given women more time on hand for themselves, family and work place; and also helped them in creating healthy home environment.

The current improved and safe means of transportation

have encouraged women to travel independently for work and pleasure.

Narrative 12

Our lifestyles have changed a lot—what our mother and grandmothers might not have experienced. I had good opportunities for education, employment, career choice, marriage choice, health care, recreation, and socialization. My parents never differentiated in providing these opportunities to us sisters (we are four) and my only brother. We never felt bias in this regard. As we sisters were growing up, I did experience parents' protective attitude towards us. They did not restrict our outside movements but we were not allowed to go out unescorted. Whereas my brother could be on his own. I do not blame them. I feel it was more because of insecure environments for women. Some segments of the society, especially the lower and uneducated were not comfortable with the newly accorded freedom to women and their coming out of home confines. They would indulge in eve teasing and sometimes even attempting rape of the lone woman. This used to be very humiliating to women.

Parents would have liked to let their daughters participate in varied social, political, economic activities; but they were always scared of the bad elements in society. They had to be cautious in this approach to protect the honour of their daughters. Those times, the social opinion was such that they would still downgrade the women for none of their faults.

Women progressed well; their progress had been creditable in spite of the social impediments. There was less gender differentiation in social opportunities. There were gender segregated schools and colleges, segregation was practiced in work environments to let women grow and feel secured. Moreover, over a period of time, even the biased segment of society has to tolerate and reconcile to women freedom of movements, access to education, recreation, employment, marriage, and inheritance etc. I am glad women of today do not suffer eve teasing. No longer there is gender segregation in schools, colleges, and work places. They play, study, grow up together, and work together. This is a very healthy development for women. At least they have gained from the sacrifices of early generations of women.

I feel more comfortable in the present social environment where people are not nosey about women's activities. Now I feel comfortable in mixed gender social mixing; as compared to my adolescent or young days.

I think in my times, as well now, parents encourage their daughters a lot to grow without any gender discrimination. Because of this, a wide variety of opportunities are now opening up to women in education, employment, and careers that were earlier men's domain. The women have to build a trust unto them to inspire confidence. The younger women have confidence. Parents would like to leave property and money for their sons after death. Inspite of inheritance laws in favour of women, my generation women do not inherit parental property or money. At times even they are asked to relinquish them willingly for the sake of family integrity. These days equal amount of money is spent on the upbringing, education, and marriages of both sons and daughters. Then why sons are preferred for inheritance? The younger generation women also face the same blocked inheritance problem.

In my generation, women were free to choose for marriage; though mainly marriages were either arranged or facilitated by parents. In 50's society was also getting ready for acceptance of 'divorce' in marriage. It was an added element facilitating women independence. Old marriage laws were being reformed to give better social status to women and Divorce was one such law. In early days, society never gave good social status to divorcee nor approved divorcee remarriages. Judiciary was protective and freedom giving to women in this regard but it was slow. The whole process of divorce could take many years and women were always the looser at the end. All said and done broken families were traumatic experiences for women those days. Therefore, women use to tolerate tortures, physical and mental cruelty, or would commit suicide rather than to break families. That was sad.

In 90's divorce has new connotation and social acceptance. Men and women can divorce on mutual incompatibility clause. They have quick mutual divorce and out of court settlements, and can remarry. This is accepted by the society. The couple has respectable place in society. This is healthy trend.

Widows were tolerated and treated as human beings in my mother's generations and mine. Though in my grandmother's time widows were treated inhumanly and were deprived physically, socially, and emotionally. Child widows used to be common phenomenon because of child marriages, high mortality rate, and even wide gap between the ages of husband and wife. In my times widows would usually live with the parents even if they would have children and be economically independent. They needed a safe and protective place in the society. The society is ready to give them a status if she is in the protection of parents, brothers, relatives. The in-laws would normally severe all relations once their son dies. Otherwise no social stigma was attached to widows or any social discrimination shown. At times superstitions are associated with widows. Otherwise now widows would dress in colored clothes—no longer dressed only in whites as was done earlier, wear jewelry, participate in social functions like any other woman participants—married or unmarried, and would interact socially also.

Parents also encouraged widow remarriages. Though it used to become difficult to remarry widows with children. But on the whole since widows had a respectable social status they were also not keen to remarry unless in dire circumstances such as being very young, not able to take care of herself, and not economically independent. I became widow at the age of thirty only. I had a small daughter. I was economically well off, and I had the protection of my parents since they were willing to live with me. I wanted to remarry but not just anybody because I was a widow. I could only remarry at the age of forty that too a widower with three grown up children. Though this was not a suitable match by all standards but I had been keen that my child should grow up with a father role model. I do not know whether that was the right step or not. But it did provide me and my daughter emotional security and a good father role model to her.

There was more sanctity attached to religion by my mother and grandmothers. They tried to emulate those religious values in their lives. Of course the compulsory and time consuming religious rituals could become tedious at times. There was more emphasis on rituals and myths rather than religious education *per se.* In older generations widows used to take cold baths at dawn and would spend many hours reading Holy Scriptures, saying prayers at home. The argument given was that such purification of thoughts would help sublimate their sexual desires. Moreover, this would be healthy pastime for them. This argument does not hold well any longer; since women are involved in many family and extra family activities inside and outside the homes. They have multiple roles to play in the society. For me religion is a way of life with honest values and without any compulsions of observing rituals.

I can visualize my daughters and daughter-in-law growing differently. Since we got ample opportunities to grow; we in turn encouraged them to grow. In addition, they have our guidance about the pitfalls of the women's newly won freedom experiments of our times.

As compared to us, today the younger generation has greater global audio and visual media exposure; whereas our exposure was limited to national influences only. Radio and television were limited to national channels only till 80's; and newspapers gave limited global exposure. Wider global exposure has created more awareness and knowledge about the world around them and greater impetus to adopt some of the global trends. The advancement in media technology, and technology in general whether related to household, medical, or transportation has certainly improved living conditions for women across generations. Science and technology has contributed to development of women.

In generations back to 1900, women have been active in politics but rarely. Women have participated actively in the freedom struggle of India and later also we had a woman Prime Minister Indira Gandhi for several years. Her efforts contributed in giving quality of life to women to a greater extent. We have women ministers who have been actively voicing the concerns of women. Women National Commission has been focusing on social and legal reforms and rights for women. Now more and more women are participating in politics with community service orientation. They are giving voice to millions of unheard women who need to be heard for redress of their grievances, and to be in the mainstream of development.

The activating factors to change the lifestyles of women in my generation were global influences, wider impact of modernization through both national and international media growth, and girls' education. British urban influence in India, freedom of India, and the Political Will of the national leaders created awareness among women of their needs, rights, and the necessary legal support through legislation. In my mother's time, the social activism of male and female reformers contributed in changing women's lifestyles for better. My daughter generation has not only benefited more from legislation protecting women, but along with that they have high social support for it. The postmodernity technology, the global media influences, low segregation in school, colleges, and work places, and low gender discrimination in social set ups have all created ambience for factually tolerating independence of women.

In retrospect, the critical incidents that changed my life were being widow at young age, then remarrying, and later having a good social status and acceptance in the second marriage family. My mother's life changed for better through British influence in India for women reforms.

Whereas my daughters generation is creating better lives for themselves through professional education, choice of wider professions, and the freedom to choose marriage partner.

Narrative 13

At this juncture of life I am bored and little depressed when I look at today's generation bubbling with enthusiasm and achieving in many directions of life. I feel I have missed the race by being nonproductive in my life.

My parents encouraged us three sisters to be highly educated and opt for work before marriage. But none of us worked after marriage as we had a well-settled life. Our husbands were earning well, and we always thought there was no economic necessity to work. This has been the usual wrong approach of well off upper class women. They merely waste their time and life in idle pursuits instead of positive contributions to society.

I do feel good about my achievements in raising my family of four children well and settling them in life. Now when they are gone and settled in their own family units; I feel the void and vacuum in life, as my husband is very busy in his profession. It is too late and not that easy to pick the early threads now. On hearing so much being talked about technology; I joined computer courses but I found it was all beyond me. I tried my hand on other fields such as travel, and organizing conferences etc. But I failed. I felt I am only good at managing house well. But the only point is that with just the two of us, the house does not need that much of time and attention.

I suggest while growing, women should pursue some professional interests along with performing family duties. In their 60's when they have more time to themselves; they can pursue those interests without gap. They can reorient themselves, and further develop those interests. This could be very satisfying. Otherwise women can feel miserable.

I have encouraged my daughter and daughter-in-law to work after marriage because of my experiences. They should combine well their housewifery, and mother's duties along with it. I still consider those are their primary duties. My contention is one gets wider perspective of life, people, and problems when working in outside home environment. Such a perspective could be challenging and give meaning to one's life. You can keep update pace with changes in society when you move out of the confines of the home.

When I was growing up, I did not face much gender discrimination for education, careers (of course the choices were limited), and marriage. May be this happened because my parents were educated (though my mother never worked), enlightened, and urbanite. But there were other girls around me who could not go for higher education however brilliant they were. Their families wanted to spend on sons' education; it was thought to be an investment, as sons would give their earnings to the family.

Some of these women could go only for protective jobs such as working in women groups, teaching in girls' school, doing tailoring and embroidery jobs from home. They had limited choices for marriages also. I felt they were constrained. They were much more constrained after marriage when they had to live a low profile life while living with in-laws. If I look back, I think women of my generation were growing in two parallel ways—open, and constrained.

I do not know how compared to us, my mother and grandmother life was balanced or happier than life of my generation. Their life pattern was mainly—an early marriage at the age of fourteen, raising large family of 7-8 children, running a good home, and a husband who would not interfere with the house running. But husband will be an authority in all other matters pertaining to family such as education, employment, and marriages of children, interaction with other relatives, family finances, and investments etc. They had no self-identity at home or outside home. They were seldom allowed to move out of home unescorted for fear of sexual harassment.

They could not have even media identity as most of them had no access to Newspaper. Radio and Television had not come on the scene. Their major past time was to indulge in arts, crafts, culinary art, and saying prayers. Gossiping with women members of the extended family who were living together in the same house was other time occupying interests. I think those days it was boon for women to live in extended families. Otherwise loneliness could have driven them crazy. Those days men use to live in men's quarters away from women. They would come home for dinner or sleep with wife. Most of their winning, dining, and male social networking would be done at male quarters. They hardly shared life with their wives and children.

I am glad my generation shares life with husbands. The husbands share time and effort in bringing up children. The younger generation is still better than we are in this respect. They have more sharedness and cooperation with husbands and children. That is why she is able to discharge effectively her multi-roles of professional earning member, homemaker, wife, mother, and active member of the community. Sometimes I feel younger women create self-stress for themselves. For them what is this life if not full of tensions—it is boring otherwise!

My generation of women have a hypocrite attitude towards life. They will not tell the truth about many things in life for fear of social disapproval. But women of today are open, straightforward, and not hypocrite about upper class morality. They have 'do not care' attitude towards social disapproval. They are assertive and aggressive and demand self-identity. Actually they are the trendsetters whether it is food, dress, music, attitudes, and social behaviour etc. And they do not want to be conventional in these respects. Whereas in our times we would be conventional in dress and behaviour (to be socially approved), however we might suffer in the process.

We did eat good food but less healthy food. Younger women are very nutrition and fitness conscious. Focus is more on nutritious food for self and family, physical exercises, personal grooming to look good. That is why, when these days you happen to visit any beauty parlor, you may find more of young women there getting all spruced up from head to toe. They use a lot more of cosmetics. In our generation it was, only occasional visit to the beauty parlor. But my mother and grandmother would have unheard of beauty parlors. They used to take care of their personal grooming at home through indigenous herbal treatments such as turmeric and milk cream for facials, henna for hair color, bark of tree for red lips, Amla for lustrous hair, manual household chores for physical exercise. Those days electric household appliances were not available. They would groom themselves decorously with lots of flowers for festivals and weddings. The focus was on use of 'nature' products.

Since my generation, women are being protected more and more by legislation. The focus is on the development and equity of women, and recognizing her as a useful member of the society. Marriage laws, inheritance laws, equal wages, and employment laws—all these give them wider opportunities to grow. Women no longer have to suffer the indignities of bigamy or polygamy, of unsuccessful marriages, and gender biases at work.

She can inherit her husband's money and property; and is not on the road when he dies. Earlier, male members of the family only inherited her husband's Provident Fund, Gratuity, and Pension (Social Security money) including immovable property. Now she has the first right over it even if it is not willed to her. She inherits her parent's property equally with her brothers. Though even now parents want sons to inherit; if they leave property for daughters; the sons squabble over it. In the interest of family integrity, it is always the daughter who will give up her rights. She will sacrifice and suffer. The inheritance laws have given her economic security.

Women of today can remain single or remarry (even when they have children) if they choose. Widows and divorcees have social status. There is hardly any social stigma to it these days. But in my times remarriages of divorcee was rare, widow remarriages with children were rare too. There was legal sanction to it but social support was coming up slowly; and the women those days were not courageous enough to do it how much they wanted. But economic independence and opportunities, professionalism, and working initially with men outside home were the factors that stimulated them to take these decisions eventually.

In my times, women have started working in different professions though choices were limited. There was not much gender discrimination at work places but there was rather segregation of sexes such as reserved tables for women in office canteens and women office rooms.

Wherever there was mixed male-female workforce, male bosses or colleagues sexually exploited the women. For men, women working in such environment were a novelty. They assumed that women were working only out of economic necessity, and they could lure them by easy money. That is why in those days women preferred, and felt secure to work in women predominated professions. Parents and husbands also allowed them to work in secure work environments. Initial segregation at work places did provide security at work places. The employers and the legislators protected them since they wanted more and more women to join the workforce.

Now the trend has changed. There is no segregation, right from schools to work places and in allied professions. Women can handle sexual exploitation better now at work places, and in public places. We hear less of eve teasing (molestation). Women handle it aggressively so males are afraid to indulge in it.

Religion was an important part of women's life in older generations. It was a mind focusing activity for them and brought solace to them. It was like sharing their lives with God. The many festivals and rituals afforded unwinding of SELF amidst the constraints of life. Now the times have changed and so too the connotation of religion for women. My generation preferred saying prayers at home, participating in few festivals and religious gatherings, and following essential rituals and rites such as at weddings and deaths. The religious practice is more in moral convictions. Younger women of today have a philosophical and practical attitude towards religion. For them morality is person specific and is in practicing good human values. They presume that festivals are mainly for getting together and they are no longer necessary for unwinding oneself socially.

Now more and more women are participating in politics. They demand the opportunities for the same. The older generation participation in politics used to be a lifetime mission for them and for a social cause. Only one in thousands could do it. Now participation in politics is must, if women want to be heard, and to have their rights protected. It is looked up as service to their own cause. Polity and community service is a must these days.

The technology whether for home or at work place is advancing and is making life comfortable and easier for women. Women are willing to go for them if they can afford. They have become necessities rather than mere luxuries. The older generations did not have the advantage of some of the advance technology nor that fitted in their lifestyles. Still they would not have grudged the fans and electricity, the tap water, and the cooking gas!

The activating factors to change women lifestyles and social values across generations have been modernity, education, employment, media influences, legislation, social activists, and Political Will.

The critical incident in my life that changed my lifestyle was when my children were settled away from home; the void thus created made me feel lonely. Since I have not prepared myself to do any productive work outside home, I felt depressed. My mother felt helpless and withdrawn after the death of her husband and her whole lifestyle changed. Earlier, her life had revolved around her husband only. Life felt empty when he passed away.

Narrative 14

I have been a homemaker and have raised two children. I have comfortable home. But I had no say in raising the children. My husband had the dominant say in disciplining them, in choosing education, career, marriage and even selecting the social circle for them. I was totally side tracked. I did resent it in the beginning but later gave in after realizing that he was happy when he was the master runner of the family.

As I was growing up in my parental home and even after marriage; I had the freedom to grow and move freely in the society. There was free gender mixing at homes, in schools, colleges, and society in general. But what I missed most was the freedom to choose my lifestyle, ways, and values of life. First, it was my father, then it was my husband who dictated my life. In our Indian society, most of the women have to lead that kind of life. Quite likely, sons may even dominate them in their old age. Women have to suffer male domination at all times.

I had my education and training for teaching from abroad. I always wanted to work but my husband never allowed me. Interestingly he always had cordial relations with his female colleagues. I had worked for four years in college before marriage. My parental family never objected. In decades of 50's and 60's many women have started working in many fields. There was policy of gender segregation in these work places in order to respect privacy of women and protect them from any sexual harassment. Women did not resent it. Later the barriers of segregation started breaking as aftermath of co-education in schools and colleges in 60's. There was less gender discrimination in academia for merit recognition and promotions. Whereas in corporate and other government offices women had to struggle hard for merit recognition and promotions.

Younger generation has enjoyed better education, and career opportunities mainly because of parental education and open attitude to life; and the wider opportunities created and available world-wise. They are more individualistic, self-confident, and ready to face competition and challenges. These days every woman wants to work—volunteer or otherwise. She feels stagnated at home, and feels she has very low productive interaction with the outside world.

These days women are getting health and fitness conscious. They enjoy facilities for outdoor sports and recreation. In my days women could only have indoor recreation. As young girls they might play in school some outdoor games and do physical exercises. But physical fitness was never a way of life. That is why in those days women would be shapely when they were young. They would loose their body figures, as they grew older, get married, and have children. Only they would get very little physical exercise from doing household chores. They considered these chores boring if not drudgery. These days most of the household chores are done electronically and automated. Moreover, they also consider household routines drudgery since women have better utilization of their time. Every effort is made by market forces and technology advancement to reduce this drudgery.

Presently, marriage choices are restricted less by caste, community, regional and nationality. The barriers started breaking as I was growing up. There is less respect for marriage as an institution. There is low incompatibility between couples. There is more sexual permissiveness in the society; more women indulge in extra marital relationships. Legal sanctions of divorce help women to break the unhappy marriages. The divorce rate is ever increasing. There is no longer social stigma attached to divorce, and remarriages of divorcees and widows.

Even society is more tolerant of widows these days. They have social status and enjoy normal life. I feel my generation struggled hard against the inequalities and social violence to women. In the end, they did gain in getting legal and social approval for divorce, widow remarriage, and inheritance.

Women have still to achieve a better place for themselves in the society. They have to be more assertive and aggressive about their rights. These days even women are frequenting courts of justice to demand their rights; whether it is in the matter of marriage, inheritance, property, and even discriminations at work place. Her motto is 'I will not tolerate social injustice any more. I will not break and bend. I will achieve on equal footing.' Such an attitude is showing far-reaching results.

FIFTH GENERATION WOMEN

Group 3: Narrative 15

Age Group 25+

I grew up in open and healthy home environment, which was conducive to my well-balanced growth. I grew up as assertive though not aggressive but gentle woman. I was achievement oriented from childhood and my parents encouraged that among all their children without any gender discrimination. I have two older brothers. My parents encouraged my participation in art, cultural, and academic competitions. They even encouraged me to go abroad alone as a teenager for international cultural competition. I enjoyed freedom of movement as I grew up. My parents trusted me. I grew up in an environment where there was free gender mixing from the very beginning of life. Children would grow up playing together, co-education in school, play and work together, there was social and professional gender inter-mixing. My parents trusted me. Only they had set the boundaries; and I believe they are necessary for disciplined behaviour.

My parents facilitated my marriage through a matrimonial advertisement in the newspaper. I approved the person and went steady with him for a while after engagement. He is highly educated and well placed but very male chauvinistic. He cannot tolerate my outshining him professionally. I am quite independent professionally and run my own placement agency. I am doing well and I make good money. But I have never tried to downgrade him. Still I cannot see why he feels insecure and inferior when I achieve better professionally. He insists on my winding the business and just to be a housewife. I refused since it was a blow on my self-esteem. Where he hurts me most is when he refuses to plan to have children. I want to have a happy home with husband and children. I persuaded and argued with him (I did not want interference in this regard from my parents or his parents), and tried to solve the issues. I did not wind up my business. I want children, and balance my work and family. We have been married for six years. On the surface we were happy but tensions were building up because of these two major issues. I decided to separate. I hoped if we live separately for a while, he will come to his senses and be amenable on both the issues.

In India, parents are always eager to counsel through intervention in such delicate matters. I prefer not to drag them in. Even our close friends did counsel us discreetly. Since friends belong to our generation, they understand our ego problems better than parents do, so they were welcome to counsel. In fact, in India we have hardly any practicing marriage counsellors in urban areas. Family is the main catharsis agent in this respect. I also support legal and social sanction of divorce. But one should not break marriages on flimsy grounds nor drag on through marriage if it is not going to work. We Indians attach great sanctity to marriage institution. Divorce should be settled mutually and amicably and not dragged in courts.

Both my parents and in-laws families are well off. My parents did give good dowry. At wedding there was no demands from my in-laws but later on they made dowry as an issue and criticized my family and me. They were never happy whenever my parents would give them customary gifts. I felt humiliated and put my foot down. I am not in favour of dowry at all even as a customary practice. But if parents can afford it, not only it makes them happy, but also it facilitates setting the couple in life. It becomes evil when there is coercion and forced demand. Dowry was legally banned due to cruel burning of brides. I welcome the ban.

But more social awareness and sanctions are needed to deal with this problem. Women cells set up by the government and many NGOs (non-government organizations) have been consistently and successfully handling it. Women themselves have to be aggressive also to deal with dowry menace. Marriage laws give them protection against many marriage problems. The compulsory registration of marriage, divorce laws, widow remarriage, her consent being the legal validity to marry, banning Sati etc. protected women against much of physical and mental cruelty. Inheritance laws have further protected her; she could inherit her husband property and money compulsorily. Even husband is not allowed to Will it to any other person. She could inherit her parental property and money. In older generations of my grandmother and foremother, they would be on the road if the husband died. Since all the money was inherited by the close male kin. It depended on the goodness of that relative how he would take care of her or her minor children. She was definitely dependent. Older generations had to face the consequences of child marriages and polygamy. Those days women were deserted at the whims of men.

The efforts of our government had gone a long way to make life easier and livable for women. We women too have to resent violence, cruelty, and subjugation. We must fight against these consistently. We must preserve our human dignity.

I personally think children are necessary for a family. Our country's population is so large that zero rate of growth should be practiced for some time. But that is not humanly possible. Children are essential for marriage since they cement the marriage relationships and keep the sanity of marriage. I believe in two children family. I have no particular preference for begetting son or daughter. Children must be given quality upbringing. This generation is likely to be more informed citizens because of wider opportunities afforded by technology and global inter-connectivity. I am glad that my generation and even my mother's generation could plan birth of children due to advancement in medical technology. Health of women in previous generations suffered in birthing a large number of children and raising a large family. The quality of the life suffered for the large families. It also created overpopulation problem for the country. Now-a-days we have better health care facilities for the women. This has been possible due to progress in medical technology, creating awareness among women about health and hygiene, changing their attitudes and behaviour for better health. Moreover, concerted efforts are made to give them access to these health facilities. But still much is desired about preventive health measures. Preventive is more important than curative. Much cleanliness is desired in the public hospitals that are visited by the masses both as indoor and outdoor patients.

Lifestyles such as dress, food, and social interactions have changed. Attitudes, beliefs, and our ways of thinking have changed. I would say all this is influenced by the process of social change and modernization. The indexes of modernization *viz.* education, media exposure, urbanization, have affected the lives of women. We are exposed to global media and to certain extent that too influence us.

The critical incidents in my life were three: marriage through matrimonial advertisement. This may give you wider choice but in my opinion not the right way for matchmaking. Two, when I decided to set up my own business. Third, when I had to separate from my husband due to lack of incompatibility. The three incidents put together changed my perspective to life.

Narrative 16
Age 30+

I am happily married with two young children. I am quite highly educated and have ambition to give high professional education to my son and daughter. I will not discriminate. It depends on their interests and capabilities. I am working as a teacher. I am working more for professional interest, and economic independence rather than for economic necessity. Being in a profession gives you self-confidence and self-identity. My husband never objected to my working. But initially my parents-in-law objected. They wanted to be assured that children and home should be looked after well if I go out to work. I took to teaching that needed few and flexible working hours and I could coordinate with my children school hours later on. I had hard time convincing my in-laws. But I won in the end and they are happy as the children and house is looked after well. I only started working when children started going to pre-school.

My father always encouraged me and my sister to go for higher studies and work. But he was very dominating. We had no choice about what courses to study and where to work. My whole personality was suppressed by his domination. Neither my husband nor my in-laws are dominating. I really achieved a lot after my marriage. But otherwise I had good childhood. In our home I never experienced any gender discrimination for education, work or for anything. We had freedom to interact with male friends but only in mixed groups. My father was the decision-maker in the family and his say was the final. But he never objected when my older sister wanted to marry person of her own choice. He organized her marriage on grand scale. My marriage was arranged and facilitated by him but he never wanted to hurry me into marriage. Rather he encouraged me to go steady for few months and know my future husband. He was very liberal in this respect. He always taught us to be honest, good, and follow religious and family values, and belief in simple living. Such training gave us good grounding in life. Though as me and my sister were growing up as independent women after marriage; we resented his running our lives and that created many family rifts.

My mother did suffer because of my father's dominating personality. She has all the comforts of life but she has no say in what she wants for herself or for her children. She is complete non-entity. In her young life she was very compliant to my father. But now seeing me and my older sister leading independent lives; she feels frustrated. She has no choice now she cannot assert herself. She is 70 plus years.

I am teaching in an international school where there is mixed faculty. I do not experience any gender discrimination in work, pay, or social behaviour. In my family, both my husband and me share decision-making. But many times I make major decisions about children education, recreation activities, and their upbringing. I take my own financial decisions, and about social dealings with my parental family. We always respect and cooperate with each other's decisions. We enjoy our family holidays together.

These days many women opt for divorce because of incompatibility. That is understandable. But I do not approve of breaking marriages on frivolous grounds. Whole family suffers due to divorce. In India marriage is not between man and woman but between families. I am in favour of widow remarriage especially of young widows. They may be economically independent but they need companionship and emotional security. They do need social status to lead normal family life. In Indian society, women without husbands do not enjoy any status however affluent they may be. My mother was a young widow with one child when she remarried my father. Initially, my father's family did not approve of it. But my father took good care of her and her child. Later, his family accepted her when other children were born and she was much respected.

I am quite religious by nature. I am not so much into observing religious rituals. I believe in practicing religious values, reading religious books, and visiting temples. I feel this gives you good focus in life. This religious bend developed in childhood as my parents practiced it. My in-laws respect my religious attitudes. My mother-in-law and sister-in-law like to attend religious gatherings more often. But I have neither any inclination nor time for them.

These days many women are active in politics. It is good that they are on the forefront; since they can voice their issues and concerns better. I feel that more and more women should be active in social and community affairs that will give them still stronger voice.

Narrative 17
Age 30+

Everyday I am growing in age and life means more misery, unhappiness, and loneliness. A sense of frustration dawns on me. I had a secured childhood growing up with three sisters and a brother. My parents are quite understanding. We have close family relationships. Parents educated us all very well and allowed us to choose the career we wanted. There was no discrimination between the sons and daughters. One of my sisters joined family export business, another sister set up a travel agency.

I am the oldest child. My parents gave us guidance and freedom to choose our marriage partners. My other three sisters and brother choose on their own and are happily married. They married outside the community; but my parents never objected to it. Since I did not have anybody in view; my parents facilitated my marriage. The match was suggested by one of our close relative. Apparently it was a good match, the person belonged to respectable and wealthy family, and he is educated, well settled in life, and good looking. But my luck did not favour me. He was sadistic. He took me on a world honeymoon trip but he used to physically abuse me and beat me with leather straps at night. Since I was away from home, all I could do was to tolerate this physical and mental cruelty while travelling.

Back home, the beatings continued. His mother asked me to put up with cruelty for the sake of other comforts of life. His father was not alive. She would not let me go out of the house and would lock me. She will not let me meet my people. My mind revolted against such cruelty. After a couple of months when one day I was beaten very badly and my body was all blue and black. I could tolerate it no more. Late in the evening with no money with me I quietly slipped out of the house, took a cab to my parents' home. They live in the same town but a few miles away. Everybody was shocked. Friends and relatives tried to intervene and patch up. Since he was a psychological case, I refused to go back and filed a divorce case in the court. I also filed with the government women cell for physical cruelty and harassment. Women cell was not much help. It is just farce. Government spent so much money on it. I wish it should play stronger role. After few months divorce was decided out of the court. Groom's side returned my clothes, jewelry, and provided me one time alimony. But this was done on one condition that I would not talk about his being sadistic as they want to remarry him. They did remarry him to a poor girl who would tolerate the physical and mental cruelty for the sake of material gains and not complain. As if poor people do not have human feelings! This whole drama of marriage divorce etc. was a traumatic experience for me. Shocking point was that mother-in-law being a woman herself was a party to such cruelty.

I got back to my job. It was great solace. My office people were very supportive. I was economically independent and continued living with my parents. They were very supportive. As society is still not supportive of divorcees and also I was quite young; my parents wanted to remarry me. It was not easy to get remarried in Indian society. Only persons with disability or minus points were ready to marry me and as if obliging me by doing so. I decided not to get married. Years rolled by. As luck would have it, I remarried a widower with two small children. He was well settled in life. The marriage was facilitated through friends. But I was not to be happy. His widowed sister was living in the family. She used to harass and give me physical beatings. He was a busy businessman. On my complaints, he would say he had no time to intervene. I have to cope up with his sister's behaviour. This was very humiliating. I decided to walk out and lead my own life. It was a mutual divorce. I questioned myself—why have I to get married? To be humiliated and be miserable!!

I am working. I am living with my parents who are also growing old. I have setup my own social network of male and female friends. I will never marry again in whatever way the society may react. I do not care any more about the society. I want to have my life and go around with anyone I like but not marry again. Society will not understand the pain of rejection and humiliation.

Legally, there is protection and sanction for divorce though social support is not that much. The fear of legal support does create better support for women. I wish drastic steps should be taken to strengthen the women crime cell. May be women from good families can volunteer to work for the cell to give humane and sympathetic touch when women and families walk in to get redress. At present the handling approach is so shabby and crude that it adds on to your torture.

In my grandmother and great grandmother's time when divorce was not legally sanctioned; women used to put up with all kinds of cruelty and suffer through teens to old age and die there. In those days, parents were neither supportive to give shelter to them if they suffer; not they were economically independent to take care of themselves. It was sheer waste of human life. In dire situations, women would either commit suicide or run away from home to be lured in prostitution. I am thankful to government and societal efforts that times have changed for women. The crucial point is—that women are getting opportunities for education and freedom to grow.

While growing up I did not experience gender discrimination socially. In work places there was no gender bias for socialization, work assignment, and wages but there was gender bias when promotions were considered. Yes it was always the male who was considered first. Over a period of time, women are getting aggressive, assertive and bonding together in work place to get what they deserve, and they are winning. My mother's generation had to work still harder to gain promotions. In those times, her male colleagues labelled any woman who was assertive and aggressive at work place as woman of loose morals in order to downgrade her. Women of those generations really struggled hard and laid ground for us. These days at least there is no restrain on gender intermixing at work places. There is no segregation or downgrading. At present there is no sexual harassment in work place whereas earlier generations were humiliated by such overtures.

Better health care facilities are available to women now. There are qualified women doctors to treat them. But my generation is open to consult a male doctor if need be. In general women are improving in health, as well they are becoming more and more health and fitness conscious.

At present there are many gimmicks and exploitation in the name of religion. Therefore, it is best to practice good values and pray at home whichever deity you worship and believe in charity giving, and community services. Rituals and festivals have lost their religious fervor. I observe them according to time and money available. It is more for social entertainment.

Progress in technology worldwide has created efficient communication networks for work, home, entertainment, and leisure. It has changed entirely the lifestyle philosophy of women particularly.

The critical incidents that changed my lifestyle and attitude towards humanity were marriage—remarriage—and the two divorces.

Narrative 18
Age 35+

I grew up over-dominated by my father in choosing everything in life—studies, career choice, food, mode of dress, and even choosing friends and husband. I appreciate parental guidance in these matters but not domination. It stifles one's personality. My father stifled my mother's personality also by over-domination. My mother is highly educated and has professional education but he never allowed her to work; as he did not want any other man to dominate her (that is what he reasoned). He was the decision-maker and took everything in his own hands. Now when he has passed away she felt so helpless in handling the outside world, her finances, and any other day-to-day normal complications of life. Since she is educated, she gained confidence to get quick grasp of the situations. But in my grandmother and great grandmother's times women were not educated, they had negligible interaction with the outside world; the death of the husband use to leave them helpless, penniless (however rich he may be), and at the mercy of the male members of the family. If son would be minor, other male relative would take over and provide the family food, clothing, and shelter.

I am glad things have changed for women. In general, my mother's generation is legally protected when her husband dies. She inherits his assets, some compulsorily like provident fund, pension, and one residence for herself. Other she would inherit by his willingness to provide other property and cash for the family in the event of his death. At least in such cases woman is in control of herself and her children's future; and not dependent on the whims and mercy of any other male. Opportunities for education, employment, information, and awareness of and interaction with the outside world give them confidence.

When I married, my husband wanted to dominate me; though both of us are professional doctors and are making equally good money. In fact he was stifling my personality by his domination. He did not want me to work though even professionally I am more qualified than him. My mind revolts against his attitude and behaviour. As a result we are having lot of rifts in our marriage. At one time even we considered divorcing each other. But we are dragging with commuter and unhappy marriage for the sake of our only child. In retrospect I think it is better to break the relationship rather than to drag. I think child rather develops insecure feelings. I am very concerned about my daughter who is extra brilliant. I feel helpless in this matter. I think my husband has to change his attitude towards women in general if he wants this marriage to work.

Personally, I am in favour of divorce if there is incompatibility. But somehow we Indian women let our marriages drag on in spite of the fact that we have won our rights legally and with lots of social support and sanction. My mother's generation had legal protection against marriage but very low social sanction and no social support. Generations earlier to her never had any legal or social provisions if marriages failed. Those days they suffered a lot and they developed fatalistic attitude towards marital bliss.

I did not experience any gender discrimination for education, careers, or marriage choice both at home and at society level. As I was growing up, I found wide opportunities and choices equally opening up for women. They were equally competing with men to gain access to them. I got the opportunity to pursue medicine, and my family supported it. Families and social times are supporting it, and they are ambitious of and are encouraging women to achieve higher. There is less gender discrimination for work assignments, wages, and promotions at lower levels in work places. Men are hard to accept women's merits for promotions and equal work assignments in senior positions and professions. There is stiff competition to achieve it. Aggressively, and assertively they push and make it many times, if they fail they are very frustrated.

My parental family is quite religious, they are strict about observing ritual and religious festivals. They hold daily prayer meetings in the evenings. I grew up in that environment; so these religious ways have become second habit to me. What I feel good about it is that early religious environment has taught me honest values of life and given stability in personality. I feel religious discipline is good for women whether older or younger generations. Only point is that it should come from within and not to be imposed.

Women social activists and community workers have been taking up women's causes and concerns to improve quality of life for them. But we need more women for voluntary community participation so they have strong say in matters that concern them such as residential environment, cleanliness, price rise, and children's schooling, and recreational activities etc. The higher concerns of social reformers have always been to get women a dignified position in society. To achieve that women do need a voice in the political system where they are negligibly represented, their concerns are either ignored or given low priority, and even seen through men's eyes.

The critical incident in my life is the marriage incompatibility; and the resentment I built against male domination—from my father to my husband. The resentment and incompatibility have both changed my personality and attitude towards marriage and life in general.

REFERENCES

Bahadur Kalim, *Equality is Still a Dream for Pakistani Women,* India Abroad Weekly, New York, April, 1997.

Carolyn Heilburn, *Wisdom of Growing Old,* 1997.

Women Conference, New Delhi, Feb. 1996.

Iqbal Ansari, "Personal Law and Women's Rights," *Hindustan Times*, New Delhi, Feb. 1997.

Karl Weick, *Sense Making in the Organizations,* Sage Publications, California, 1995.

Leonard Mary, *Where Feminism Began,* The Boston Globe, July 16, 1998.

Narula Uma, "Women Ignored Factor in Development," *Mainstream*, New Delhi, 1988.

——, *Broken Homes: Compelling Causes and Socio-domestic Implications,* Social Welfare, New Delhi, 1967.

——, *Aspirations of Indian Working Women,* Social Welfare, New Delhi, 1967.

——, *Science & Technology for Hilly Women: A Communication Perspective,* In Eds. Anjali Bahuguna & Uma Narula, Har Anand Publishers, New Delhi, 1997.

Report, Pakistan Human Development Center, *Bias Against Women in South Asia,* April, 1997.

Report, Sakshi (NGO), *Gender and Judges: A Judicial Point of View,* Delhi, 1998.

Report, *Women and Local Politics in Mumbai and London: The Quota Innovation, 1st Part,* All India Institute of Local Self Government Mumbai and East London Business School 1996.

Research Study, *Gender Bias in Indian Civil Services,* Lal Bahadur National Academy of Administration, Mussoorie, 1998.

Research Study, *TISS Special Cell, Tata Institute of Social Sciences*, Mumbai, 1998.

Research Study, *Trends in Matrimonial Litigation,* Family Courts, Mumbai, 1998.

SUBJECT INDEX